• EXPLORING RELIGIONS •

Judaism

ANNE GELDART

Heinemann

Heinemann Educational Publishers
Halley Court, Jordan Hill, Oxford OX2 8EJ
a division of Reed Educational & Professional Publishing Ltd

OXFORD MELBOURNE AUCKLAND
JOHANNESBURG BLANTYRE GABORONE
IBADAN PORTSMOUTH (NH) USA CHICAGO

Heinemann is a registered trademark of Reed Educational
& Professional Publishing Ltd

First published in 2000

04 03 02 01 00
9 8 7 6 5 4 3 2 1

British Library Cataloguing in Publication Data
Geldart, Anne
Judaism – (Exploring religions)
1. Judaism – Juvenile literature
I. Title
230

ISBN 0 431 093040

Designed and produced by Gecko Ltd, Bicester, Oxon
Illustrated by Barry Rowe, Gill Bishop and Gecko Ltd
Printed and bound in Spain by Edelvives

Acknowledgements

The author would like to thank Rabbi Forta for his
comments, and Sue Walton, Rob Bircher, Jane Tyler and
the rest of the Heinemann team for their help and
guidance. And to her husband, many thanks for his
unfailing support.

The publishers would like to thank the following for
permission to reproduce copyright material:

Lis Harris for the extracts from *Holy Days*, published by
Summit Books, a division of Simon & Schuster Inc, on p.
109; Jewish Publication Society of America, for the extract
from *Judaism and Modern Man* by W. Herberg on p. 142;
Yigael Yadin for the extract from *Bar-Kokhba,* reproduced
with permission of the publishers, Weidenfeld and
Nicolson, on p. 5.

The publishers would like to thank the following for
permission to reproduce photographs:

The Ancient Art & Architecture Collection pp. 8, 14, 60;
Peter Arkell/Impact Photos p. 117; Stephen Bolsom p. 81;
Werner Braun pp. 32, 90, 108, 129; Hans-Jurgen
Brurkard/Network Photographers p. 126; Circa Photo
Library pp. 4 (bottom left), 50; Charles Green p. 82; The
Hutchison Library p. 62; Illustrated London News p. 79;
Yehudis Ives p. 113; Rabbi Louis Jacobs p. 142; The Jewish
Education Bureau p. 84; The Jewish National & University
Library p. 10; The London Museum of Jewish Life p. 140;
Marisa & Gerard Photographers p. 75; Microscopix p. 96
(bottom left & right); Sidney Moulds/Science Photo Library
p. 97; Peter Osborne pp. 4 (middle and bottom right), 27,
31, 36, 37, 38, 40, 44, 45, 46, 49, 54, 57, 64 (both), 66
(right), 70, 71, 88, 92, 95; Raissa Page/Format Partners
p. 25; Z. Radovan, Jerusalem pp. 23, 63, 132, 136, 145,
148; John Rifkin p. 120; John Rifkin/Jewish Care p. 118;
Anat Rotem-Braun pp. 4 (top right), 102, 135; Royal
Observatory, Edinburgh/Science Photo Library p. 18;
RSPCA p. 124; Rachel Rietman pp. 43, 98; Science Photo
Library p. 96 (top right); R. Shymansky p. 76; E.
Simanor/Robert Harding Picture Library p. 29; Juliette
Soester pp. 53, 59, 66 (left), 72, 78, 87; Frank Spooner
Pictures pp. 4 (top left), 107; Andrew Syred/Science Photo
Library p. 96 (top left); Topham Picturepoint pp. 16, 100,
115, 147; B. Weinbraum p. 130; Zefa Pictures pp. 122, 151.

Cover photograph by Juliette Soester.

The publishers have made every effort to contact
copyright holders. However, if any material has been
incorrectly acknowledged, the publishers would be
pleased to correct this at the earliest opportunity.

CONTENTS

1 WHO ARE THE JEWS?

Look at the pictures below. The people do not look alike. They come from different parts of the world and speak different languages. But they are all Jews. The British schoolgirls and the American actress are **Ashkenazim**, Western Jews. The Indian secretary is an Oriental (Eastern) Jew. Oriental Jews are called **Sephardim**. Ashkenazim and Sephardim are the largest groups of Jews and this book is mainly about them.

Jewish history began about 4000 years ago. It has been a very varied history. Jews have

American actress

Yemenite couple

British schoolgirls

Ethiopian boy

Indian secretary

been free people and slaves, rulers and refugees. They have settled in their own land and spread all over the world. Jews have lived in almost every country at some time.

Jews make up only 0.27 per cent of the world's population, that is 27 Jews for every 10 000 people. However, they have greatly influenced human history. Jews have been among the best musicians, writers, scientists, business people and politicians. Also millions of people base their religious and moral codes on original Jewish teachings

This book is about Jews and their religion, Judaism. Judaism is more than a religion, it is a way of life. Not all Jews observe (follow) their religion to the same degree. Some keep some beliefs and practices and ignore others. This book deals mainly with the beliefs, practices and organizations of observant Jews.

THE JEWS AS A FAMILY

You can see from the pictures that Jews belong to many races and nations. Jews may or may not be religious. But they are all Jewish. So who are the Jews?

Most Jews do not choose to be Jewish – they are born Jewish. Because of this they think of themselves as having a special bond with other Jews, even those they have never met. Most Jews feel links with Jews of the past, and take it for granted they are descended from the ancient Israelites of the Bible.

It is doubtful whether anyone could actually trace their family back so far. However, most Jews today have Jewish parents, grandparents, great-grandparents and so on. Jews think of themselves as a family with links throughout the world. This feeling of being a widely scattered family causes Jews to try to help other Jews elsewhere who might be in trouble. Recently Jews in Britain and the USA campaigned on behalf of oppressed Jews in the former Soviet Union. Jews in Israel

arranged airlifts to rescue other Jews from famine conditions in Yemen and Ethiopia.

◇

KEY WORD

Observant Jews – Jews who follow the teachings of Judaism both by attending public worship and in their home life and private prayers

FACTFILE

Professor Yadin's discovery

In 1963 Professor Yigael Yadin, an Israeli archaeologist, found some ancient household goods in a cave near the Dead Sea in Israel. A Jewish family running away from the Romans had left them there nearly two thousand years ago.

The discovery affected Professor Yadin deeply. He described how, living in tents set up by the Israel Defence Forces, and walking every day through the ruins of a Roman camp, reminded him how the Romans had caused the death of his forefathers. Nothing remained of the Romans except a heap of stones in the desert. Yet here, the descendants of those who had fled the Romans had returned to gather up their ancestors' precious belongings.

'Remember the days of old, consider the years of each passing generation; ask your father and he will inform you, your elders and they will tell you.'

(Deuteronomy 32:7)

Jews are proud of being an ancient people. You need to know about Jewish history to understand how Jews think about themselves.

THE PATRIARCHAL AGE

Abraham and Sarah, Isaac and Rebecca, Jacob and his four wives Rachel, Leah, Bilhah and Zilpah are the three generations of Patriarchs (fathers) and Matriarchs (mothers) of the Jewish people.

The Patriarchs and their families were herdsmen. They wandered over Syria, Israel and Egypt with their cattle and sheep about 4000 years ago. They believed in one God (see page 18). They worshipped God through prayer and sacrifice and by acts of kindness and hospitality. The Bible tells how God promised the Patriarchs that the land of Canaan, now called Israel, would belong to their descendants.

During a famine, Jacob and his family went to live in Egypt where there was plenty of food. They settled there and prospered. Many years later a new king took over the throne of Egypt. He blamed the Israelites for Egypt's economic problems (see page 48) and made them slaves.

THE CALL OF MOSES

After some time, God wanted to bring the Israelites back to Canaan. He chose a man named Moses to set his people free and lead them to the Promised Land. Seven weeks

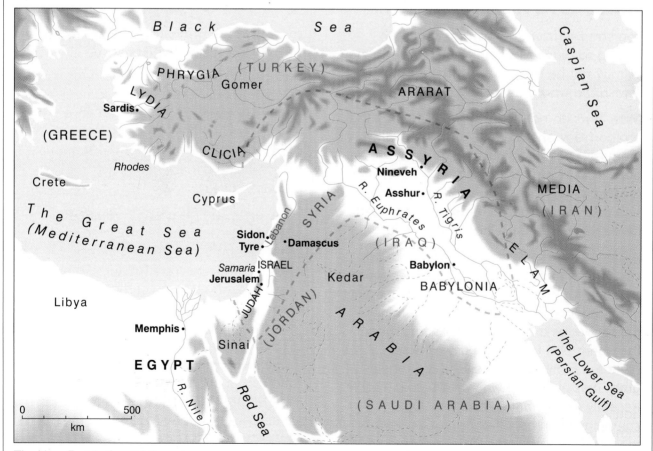

The Near East in the eighth century BCE

after leaving Egypt they reached Mount Sinai (see page 52) where God gave Moses the **Torah**.

The Torah contains God's instructions about how Jews should live. Moses taught it to the people as he led them towards Canaan. Jews still think of Moses as the greatest prophet and call him **Moshe Rabbenu**, our teacher Moses.

God told Moses to make a sanctuary or portable temple for worship. They travelled for 40 years, and Moses died within sight of the Promised Land. They were led in by his successor, Joshua.

THE TRIBAL CONFEDERACY (c. 1500–1000 BCE)

The Israelites divided the land among the twelve tribes. Each tribe had its own land and leaders who were called judges. Each tribe also had its high, holy place for worship and sacrifices. The sanctuary was the most important place of worship.

Throughout the time, enemies came to rob and plunder. The judges tried to raise armies to fight off the invaders, but usually only the tribe actually threatened would take part. In the eleventh century BCE the Philistines, who lived in the south-west, attacked. They wanted to conquer the whole of Canaan. The tribes of Israel asked Samuel, the last judge, to find them a king. Samuel chose a brave and devout man named Saul.

THE MONARCHY AND THE PROPHETS (c. 1100–586 BCE)

Saul brought the Israelites together and fought several battles against the Philistines. At first he was successful. Then he suffered a great defeat and was killed.

Saul's son-in-law, David, became king after him. He fought off the Philistines and reigned for 40 years. During this time he created a small empire. The reign of David's son Solomon was peaceful and prosperous. Great building works were carried out. Solomon replaced the simple sanctuary with a Temple that took seven years to build.

After Solomon died, the northern tribes set up their own kingdom, which they called Israel. The southern tribes formed the kingdom of Judah, with Solomon's son as king. The people of Judah became known as Jews. The two kingdoms lasted 200 years.

During the last few years of this period, the wealthy ruling classes robbed and oppressed the poor. The judges did not stop them. Great prophets arose, such as Hosea, Amos, Isaiah and Jeremiah, who feared no one. They denounced even the most powerful people.

In 722 BCE Assyria's powerful army conquered Israel and took the Israelites into exile. They were never heard of again. In 586 BCE the Babylonians destroyed Jerusalem and the Temple and led the people of Judah into exile in Babylon.

KEY WORDS

Confederacy – a political alliance

Prophet – someone to whom God reveals His will

FACTFILE

Monotheism
Monotheism means the worship of one God. The Jews were the first to recognize and worship one God.

UNDER PERSIAN RULE (538–333 BCE)

Even before the Babylonians destroyed the Temple, Jews had moved away from the Holy Land. They settled in many different countries. The settlements were called the **diaspora**, which means 'dispersion'. Babylon had the largest number of Jews of the diaspora.

In 538 BCE Cyrus the Great, King of Persia, conquered Babylon. He allowed all the exiled Jews to return home. Some of the Jews returned to Judah to rebuild the Temple. Most Jews remained in Babylon and formed a thriving community. Others returned to the Holy Land after the Temple was finished.

THE HELLENISTIC PERIOD (323–63 BCE)

By 323 BCE Alexander the Great had conquered the Persian Empire. He and his successors brought Greek culture (way of life) to the Middle East. They brought new kinds of art, literature, philosophy and government. This became known as Hellenism. Many Jews liked Hellenism and left their traditional lifestyle. Bad feelings developed between these Jews and traditional Jews. This came to a head when King Antiochus IV (175–163 BCE) tried to force the Jews to follow his laws. This led to the Maccabean Revolt (see page 56) when the Jews set up their own monarchy.

ROMAN RULE (63 BCE–c. 300 CE)

The Romans brought the Holy Land under their harsh rule in 63 BCE. Some Jews wanted to rise up against them, others wanted to live in peace.

The Jews formed many different sects (religious groups). Each had different ideas about how Judaism should be practised. Most of them thought a new leader would come. He would be God's Messiah (anointed one). There were different ideas about what

Holy objects stolen from the Temple

the Messiah would do. However, they all believed that, when he came, a new age of universal peace would begin. Several Jews claimed to be the expected Messiah. The best known is Jesus of Nazareth. His followers later formed the Christian Church.

In 66 CE one sect, the Zealots, led a revolt against the Romans. In 70 CE the Romans destroyed Jerusalem and the Temple (see page 60). In 132 CE, the Jews rebelled. They were led by Simon **Bar Kokhba**. They drove out the Romans, but in 135 CE Bar Kokhba was defeated. After that many disheartened Jews left the country to join the **diaspora**.

JEWS IN BABYLON (c. 200–1040 CE)

By about 200 CE there were Jews living in many countries. There were large communities in Rome, Egypt and Persia. The largest Jewish settlement was in Babylon. The Jews in Babylon were powerful. They helped the local kings to fight against the Romans.

During this period in Babylon, scholars wrote the **Talmud**. This is one of the most important works in Judaism (see page 31). Jews from all over the world consulted the leading scholars, or **gaonim**, on questions of Jewish law (see page 32). The last of these scholars was assassinated in 1040 CE.

THE EUROPEAN MIDDLE AGES (c. 8TH–15TH CENTURIES)

During the Middle Ages, Europe was Christian. The Church was very powerful. It was a difficult time for Jews. At times they were just tolerated, at other times they were killed. Mediaeval Christians thought the Jews were the ones who killed Christ (see page 14) and they passed harsh laws against them. Sometimes they were forced to live in walled off parts of towns, called ghettos, where they were locked in at night. They were not allowed to follow careers of their choice.

Jews were accused of many bad things – from poisoning wells to killing Christian children and using their blood in Jewish rituals. Mobs often attacked them. Some towns or countries expelled entire Jewish populations. England expelled its Jews in 1290.

Despite all this, Jewish learning prospered in Europe and in Arab countries. Jewish scholars were mainly concerned with work on the Talmud. The work of these scholars is still important today. They also wrote about the Bible and its meaning, and developed Hebrew grammar. One famous scholar was **Rabbi** Shlomo ben Yitzhak (1040–1105), known as **Rashi**.

In 1492 Spain expelled its Jewish population. Some Jews settled in Holland. Others travelled to the Holy Land. One group of scholars set up a centre for Jewish learning in Safed. Rabbi Joseph Caro, an important scholar, published a Code of Law called the Prepared Table (see page 32). Others started to explain teachings about how individuals relate to God.

THE JEWS UNDER ISLAM

Muslims were more tolerant of other religions than Christians had been. The Jews in the east were better treated than those in Europe. They could take up professions and some held high positions in government. Some Jews moved from Christian to Islamic countries.

However, Muslims never really forgave the Jews for rejecting Muhammad. There were times when they treated the Jews harshly. Under the Muslims who conquered North Africa and Spain in the twelfth century, Jews had to wear special clothing and their work was restricted.

However, as in Europe, Jewish scholarship flourished. One of the most important Jewish scholars of the time was Rabbi Moses ben Maimon (1135–1204), known as Maimonides. He wrote an important book of Jewish Law (see page 32) as well as works on philosophy.

KEY WORDS

Hellenism – the acceptance of a Greek way of life

Messiah – from a Hebrew word meaning 'anointed', or having holy oil poured over a person's head

Ritual – the actions of worship

FACTFILE

Safed

Safed is a small mountain town in Galilee that became a centre for Jewish mystics. It is one of the four holy cities in Israel, the others being Jerusalem, Hebron and Tiberias.

THE ENLIGHTENMENT IN EUROPE

The Enlightenment was an eighteenth-century movement. Scientists and scholars stressed the importance of reason in reaching decisions. They encouraged people to think again about existing ideas, especially social and religious ideas.

The English scientist, Sir Isaac Newton, showed that the movement of the planets could be explained without reference to God. Europeans discovered that China was an ancient civilization that flourished without Christianity. The Qur'an was translated into modern languages which showed that other religions could be spiritual.

Before this, people had taken the teachings of religion for granted. Now they started to work things out for themselves. They became more secular. They thought they could live without religion. This changed things for the Jews.

An Englishman, John Locke, wrote that all human beings are born equal. This made people look again at the Christian view that the Jews were a hateful race. Some people thought that if Jews had the same opportunities as others, they could become 'good citizens'. Some even talked of giving Jews the right to vote.

THE RISE OF HASKALAH

At that time, in most of Europe, the Jews lived separately. They dressed differently and spoke a different language. The laws did not allow them to work in the higher professions. This seemed to prove to some people that Jews were inferior and cursed by God.

Some Jews did learn the language of their gentile (non-Jewish) neighbours and studied mathematics and philosophy. Moses Mendelssohn was a Jew who gained respect for his powerful intelligence and his writings.

Mendelssohn and his followers thought the Jews could be liberated if they changed their lifestyle. They encouraged Jews to study other subjects as well as the Bible and **Talmud**. They said Jews should learn European languages and stop writing all their business records in Hebrew. They should train for agriculture and crafts. This move to make Jewish live like their gentile neighbours became known as the **Haskalah** (Jewish

Napoleon's 'Sanhedrin'

Enlightenment). Those who accepted these ideas were called **maskilim**.

Some maskilim wanted to change the way Jews dressed, spoke and traded. Others wanted to change the Jewish religion. This led to the foundation of the Reform movement in Germany (see page 136).

EMANCIPATION

Some governments in western Europe were willing to grant Jews full civil rights. The French Revolution of 1789 proclaimed 'liberty, equality, fraternity' for everyone in France, including the Jews. But this was only on condition that they started thinking of themselves as French. Napoleon said that 'within ten years there will be no difference between a Jew and a Frenchman'. In 1807 he set up a **Sanhedrin** (Jewish council) because he wanted them to pass laws allowing marriages between Jews and non-Jews. The Sanhedrin agreed that mixed marriages would be valid according to French law, but not according to Jewish law.

THE JEWS OF RUSSIA

In Russia Jews were also being pressed to change. Jewish men had to serve 20 years in the Russian army. The aim of this was to convert them to Christianity. Schools were set up to make Jews more Russian. The Russian Government tried to persuade Jews to accept Christianity. Maskilim received government support for their plans to add non-religious studies in Jewish schools and spend less time on Talmud. However, most Jews remained loyal to their own people.

Jews in Russia were persecuted harshly. Thousands left eastern Europe. From 1880 onwards, they began moving to the USA, Palestine, Britain, South Africa and Australia.

THE RISE OF RELIGIOUS AND POLITICAL MOVEMENTS

During the nineteenth century, political shifts caused great changes in Jewish life. In Germany, the Reform movement tried to adapt Judaism to the needs of Jews living there. In eastern and central Europe, the Zionist movement wanted the Jews to have a country of their own. In Russia, the Bund (a Jewish socialist movement) wanted Jews to become loyal Russians.

Meanwhile the **Hasidic movement** in Poland, the **Musar movement** in Russia and neo-Orthodoxy in Germany all helped to strengthen traditional Jewish values (see pages 128–35).

KEY WORDS

Enlightenment – when a person finds they understand a new idea

Emancipation – to be set free, liberated

FACTFILE

Voltaire 1694–1778

The French writer and philosopher, Voltaire, was one of the central figures in the eighteenth-century Enlightenment in Europe. He believed that literature could help to bring about social change. His 1756 *Essay on General History and the Character of Nations* was a study of human progress. His writings stressed the need for religious tolerance. He rejected formal religion and the power of the Christian clergy, but held a strong belief in the existence of God.

Early in the twentieth century there were thousands of Jews living in the USA. In Britain there were Jewish groups living near the docklands of London, Merseyside and Tyneside, and in Manchester, Hull and Bradford. They were mainly poor, working-class people, trying to make a living and provide an education for their children.

For the Jews who were deeply religious it was a difficult time. In Britain they could not find work that gave them Saturdays (the Jewish **Shabbat** or Sabbath) and Holy Days free. In those days there was no Social Security. If a man did not work, he had no money and his family suffered. As a result, some took to working on the Sabbath and religious observance weakened.

In the 1920s and 1930s young Jews wanted to be accepted into British society. They felt embarrassed that their parents had east European accents. Many changed their names to English-sounding ones. Some 'married out', that is, married non-Jewish partners. Only a minority of Jews in London, Manchester and Gateshead remained faithful to their religion and its teachings.

THE HOLOCAUST

In 1933 Adolf Hitler and his National Socialist (Nazi) Party were elected to power in Germany. They had two aims. First they wanted to restore Germany to greatness by conquering Europe. This meant producing arms and training a huge army. Secondly they needed to find a scapegoat for all Germany's problems (see page 16). By blaming the Jews they gave the German people an object for their anger and frustration.

The Nazis claimed that the Jews controlled the banks and had all the top jobs in Germany. They said the Jews and the communists were plotting to take over the country. They began to take away the Jews' civil rights. Most of the German people agreed with this. This led to the Nazis' 'final solution of the Jewish problem' – wiping them out entirely. They built concentration camps in all the countries they conquered. During World War II six million Jews died in these camps. 1.5 million of them were children. This destruction of the Jews is known as the **Holocaust**.

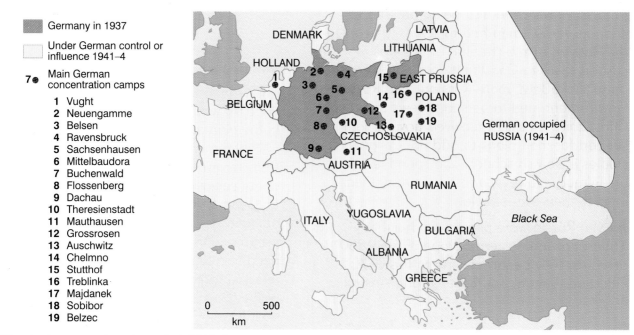

Germany in 1937

Under German control or influence 1941–4

7● Main German concentration camps

1 Vught
2 Neuengamme
3 Belsen
4 Ravensbruck
5 Sachsenhausen
6 Mittelbaudora
7 Buchenwald
8 Flossenberg
9 Dachau
10 Theresienstadt
11 Mauthausen
12 Grossrosen
13 Auschwitz
14 Chelmno
15 Stutthof
16 Treblinka
17 Majdanek
18 Sobibor
19 Belzec

The death camps where Jews died, 1941–5

THE STATE OF ISRAEL

After the war, many Holocaust survivors wanted to settle in Palestine, which was then under British rule. However, this was a slow process and Arab governments opposed it. There was hostility between the Jews of Palestine and the British authorities. In May 1948 British forces left Palestine, and the Jews declared the State of Israel (see page 63).

The Arab countries did not want a Jewish state, so they attacked Israel. The Jews fought back in the War of Independence and defeated the Arabs.

THE POST-WAR PERIOD

When the Allied armies entered the concentration camps in 1945, the whole world saw the full horror of the Nazi Holocaust. Jews in many countries were angry. They felt frustrated that they had not been able to help and vowed it would never happen again.

After the State of Israel was set up, Jews felt a new sense of pride in being Jewish. While pre-war Jews had tried to cast off Judaism, post-war Jews felt a new desire to rediscover their Jewish roots.

From 1950 onwards there was a burst of new Jewish schools and higher education centres, as well as community centres and youth movements.

JEWS TODAY

Not all Jews think the same way or believe the same things. Most support the State of Israel. They send money and people to support Israel, particularly during wars with its Arab neighbours. In turn, Israel provides refuge for Jews escaping persecution. Jews from Yemen and Ethiopia were airlifted to Israel. Thousands of Jews left after the collapse of the USSR and settled in Israel.

In Britain, Jewish life is complex. Some Jews belong to religious, social and political groups with different views. Many Jews do not become involved at all. Jews mix with non-Jews at universities, in the professions and in business. More Jews are marrying out than at any time in the past. Many Jews are worried about this.

On the other hand, nearly a third of Jewish children in the UK attend Jewish schools. Many more are involved in Jewish youth organizations. Young Jews today seem to be taking a much more active interest in their Jewish roots than their grandparents did.

FACTFILE

A Holocaust survivor remembers

We were ten kids: six boys, four girls. What's unique about us is from the ten children, nine returned from the Holocaust. The day after Passover 1944, the Hungarian police came and collected the Jews together in one district. Two weeks later we were put on the cattle trains to Auschwitz. That was my father, my mother, myself and two of my sisters. The rest came later. We went to Auschwitz separately, in a cattle car. We arrived in the dark and we were separated. We couldn't speak. I think my parents were gassed the same night.

The rest of us were in Auschwitz, and we all went through the *Gehenna*, the Hell of the Holocaust. The young ones were taken to Mauthausen after two weeks to work on tunnels for a secret factory. First we had to stand to attention for two hours in the sun. The assessor yelled, '*Yuden* (Jews), look at that chimney over there. That's the only way you can get out of here.'

(from *The Holocaust Survivor*, Dan and Lavinia Cohn-Sherbok)

Throughout history there have been people who admired the Jews and have converted to Judaism. Others have hated the Jews and tried to kill them all. Sadly, many people are hostile towards Jews. This hostility is called **anti-semitism**.

People suggest many reasons for anti-semitism. They hate Jews for being too rich – or too poor; for being communist or capitalist. Some forms of anti-semitism begin in religions. Christians believe that Jesus is the Son of God and the Jews killed him. Muslims believe Muhammad was God's final prophet and the Jews rejected him. Yet many Christians and Muslims get on very well with Jews.

In some countries, such as Poland and Germany, anti-semitism seems deeply fixed in people's minds. In Britain and the USA it crops up occasionally. Even today, people may curse or spit upon Jewish people, or damage their cemeteries. No one can find a good reason for anti-semitism.

THE ANCIENT WORLD

During their early history, Jews got on well with their neighbours most of the time. Once they moved into the Holy Land there were some periods of hostility, mainly because the Jews would not intermarry with the other tribes or eat their food.

There were occasional outbreaks of war against the Jews. For example, the Persian Grand Vizier (see pages 8 and 58) tried to kill thousands of Jews because one Jew refused to bow to him. Under Roman rule, Jews generally had a peaceful life and had certain privileges. Some Roman nobles admired Jewish morality and copied their lifestyle. Later, however, insulting stories began to circulate about the Jews. People said the Jews descended from a race of lepers.

CHRISTIAN TREATMENT OF JEWS

Christians believed that the Jews had committed the worst possible sin. They had rejected Jesus. Christians believed that Jesus was God in human form, come to save the world. If the Jews rejected Jesus, it was the same as rejecting God. Christians developed the idea that God hated the Jews. Their literature described Jews as descendants of the devil (see *John 8:44*). They said the Jews' only hope was to accept Christ and convert to Christianity.

During the Middle Ages, Christian thinkers preached and wrote disgraceful things about Jews. They taught small children that the Jews murdered Jesus. Kings passed humiliating laws against them, crusaders massacred them. Martin Luther, the Protestant reformer, wrote:

'…their synagogues should be set on fire, and whatever does not burn up should be covered or spread over with dirt so that no one may ever be able to see a cinder or stone of it. And this ought to be done for the honour of God and of Christianity…their homes should likewise be broken down and destroyed…they should be deprived of their prayer books and Talmuds…all their cash and valuables should be taken from them…God's rage is so great against them…'

Jews being burned alive – medieval woodcut

In Spain, in the fifteenth century, Jews were forced to convert to Christianity. People did not trust these 'New Christians' as they thought their conversion was not sincere (see page 46). Christians would only marry other Christians of 'pure blood'. This idea of 'purity of blood' led to the racial anti-semitism of the Nazis five centuries later (see page 16).

THE ENLIGHTENMENT

The Enlightenment thinkers believed in justice and opposed the authority of the Church (see page 10). Some of them supported the Jews who had suffered so much injustice at the hands of Christians. Others thought that Jews were superstitious and backward, and were the enemies of the modern state. This resulted in the *Judenfrage* (Jewish question) being raised every time the civil rights of the Jews were discussed.

The 'Jewish question' was this: can Jews become full Germans or French if they insist on living a separate existence, with their own set of loyalties and their own laws? People began to feel suspicious of the Jews for keeping themselves to themselves. They even viewed Napoleon's **Sanhedrin** (see page 11) as a Jewish secret society. This started the story that the Jews were plotting to take over the world.

At the same time, there was a rise in a German sense of nationhood. The Jews had no part in this. The Germans brought up old prejudices carried down from the Christian centuries. However 'German' they might seem, Jews were really aliens. They could not be German until their Jewishness disappeared.

In France, anti-semitism was also deeply ingrained. In 1894, Alfred Dreyfus, a Jewish officer in the French army, was accused of spying (see page 146). He was found guilty and sent to Devil's Island. Later, he was proved innocent and pardoned.

THE RUSSIAN EMPIRE

Jews had not been allowed to live in Russia since the fifteenth century. In 1772, when Russia conquered part of Poland, they found thousands of Jews living there. They took the inhabitants of the first Jewish village to the nearest river and drowned them. However, they could not do this with all of them, there were too many. In 1791 they decided to let the Jews live in an area stretching from Kovno to the Black Sea. This was called the Pale of Settlement. This way the Tsar's Government could prevent them from mixing with 'Holy Russia'.

The Jews living in the Pale were very poor. Many of the younger generation joined the revolutionary movements. In 1881 Tsar Alexander II was assassinated. A Jewish girl was among those responsible. A month later, stirred up by the Russian press, anti-Jewish riots called **pogroms** broke out. These pogroms spread to 160 towns and villages. Jews were killed and robbed, but the police did nothing.

In 1905 the Tsar's secret police produced a document which was supposed to contain the Jews' plans for taking over the world. It was called 'Protocols of the Elders of **Zion**'. This is used in anti-Jewish literature even today.

FACTFILE

The language of hatred

The words 'anti-semitism' and 'pogrom' first appeared in 1879 in a book called *The Victory of Judaism over Germanism*. The author was Wilhelm Marr, who wrote many books stirring up European nationalism and describing Jews as 'the enemy within'.

THE SOVIET UNION

The communist revolution in Russia took place in October 1917. Lenin, the communist leader, said that there would be no more **anti-semitism**. People who carried out **pogroms** were enemies of the revolution.

However, during the late 1920s, Joseph Stalin actively began to encourage anti-semitism. This meant he could remove Jews from positions of authority. Later Stalin condemned Israel as being an anti-Soviet state financed by the USA. During Stalin's rule Jews were accused of anti-Soviet activities. The secret police murdered thousands of Jews or sent them to Siberian labour camps. Just a few synagogues were kept, to show the rest of the world how tolerant the Soviet regime was towards Jews.

Stalin died in 1953 and was replaced by Khrushchev. The State still backed anti-semitism and Judaism was declared to be 'culturally backward'. Synagogues were closed. Jews were forbidden to gather, even in private homes for prayer. Anyone who applied for permission to emigrate to Israel lost their job.

This went on until the collapse of the Soviet Union. Under Boris Yeltsin, Russian Jews became liberated and many left to settle in Israel.

NAZI GERMANY

After the end of World War I in 1918, Germany lost twelve per cent of its land, most of its coal and steel industry, and had to pay the cost of the war. This brought massive unemployment and runaway inflation. In 1933 the National Socialist German Workers' Party (Nazi Party), led by Adolf Hitler, was elected to power.

The Nazis blamed the Jews for Germany's defeat in World War I, and for the continuing economic problems. They began to strip Jews of their citizens' rights. They removed

Nazis calling for Germans to boycott Jewish shops

Jews from all positions of authority. They imposed humiliating rules on the Jews and banned them from sports stadia and swimming pools.

They did this because they wanted Germany to be *Judenrein*, free of Jews. They even planned to transport Jews to Madagascar and use them as slaves.

In 1937 came the concentration camps. They forced Jews to work as slaves in these camps. When the Jews could no longer work, the Nazis killed them. Some were used for medical experiments. Young girls were sterilized, then forced to become prostitutes for German soldiers. The old and disabled were sent straight to the gas chambers. By 1945 six million Jews had been murdered. Jews call this the **Shoah**, or catastrophe. It is commonly called the **Holocaust**.

The Nazis justified their treatment of Jews by claiming that they themselves were the Aryan *Herrenvolk*, the master race. Jews, or Semites, were a sub-human species. The Nazis even designed a measuring system for people's heads to show whether they were Aryans or Semites.

OPPOSITION TO THE NAZIS

The ordinary German people, including most of the Christian Churches, were taken in by Nazi propaganda and accepted that Jews were an inferior race. The Confessing Church, however, opposed Nazism. About 700 of its priests were arrested.

Under German occupation, anti-semitic Poles and Ukrainians massacred their Jews. Danes and Norwegians bravely tried to save theirs. Sweden gave protection to Jewish refugees.

Some outstanding individuals risked their lives to hide Jews or help them escape. Cardinal Angelo Roncalli saved thousands of Jewish lives. He became Pope John XXIII and had all anti-Jewish references removed from the prayer book. Since then, many clergy have tried to make amends for the Church's silence under Nazism.

RECENT MOVEMENTS

Today there are neo-Nazi groups in Germany and other European countries. These consist mainly of young thugs who regard Hitler as their hero. They carry out acts of violence against non-European and disabled persons.

THE MIDDLE EAST

Jerusalem is a holy city for both Muslims and Jews. Muslims believe that Muhammad ascended to heaven from the place that was the Holy of Holies in King Solomon's Temple.

When Jews began to re-settle in the Holy Land, then called Palestine, they found a well-established Arab population. The Arabs believed the land really belonged to them. Soon there was conflict between Arabs and Jews over the occupation of the land.

Since the foundation of the State of Israel, some Arab governments have tried to destroy the Jewish state. Since the 1950s there have been three major wars. Arab governments taught that Zionism was evil and that Israel was the first step towards world domination by the Jews. The 'Protocols of the Elders' (see page 15) was translated into Arabic and taught in Arab secondary schools.

During the same time Arab terrorists attacked Jewish targets in Israel and abroad. In 1979 Israel signed a peace agreement with Egypt. In 1993 and 1994 they signed agreements with the Palestine Liberation Organization (PLO) and Jordan. However, Arab terrorist groups still commit acts of violence around the world in an attempt to destroy Israel.

FACTFILE

The Jewish Brigade

In September 1944, during World War II, The Jewish Brigade was formed as a separate unit within the British army. This followed a long struggle by the Jewish community to be allowed to fight the Nazis. Many were refugees from Europe. The Brigade had its own flag and emblem. They fought alongside British soldiers against the Nazis in Egypt, northern Italy and northwest Europe.

KEY WORDS

Concentration camps – guarded prison camps where Nazis murdered millions of Jews

Propaganda – the publishing of information for or against a group or government

The next four units are about some of the things that Jews believe about God, life and the world.

BELIEF IN ONE GOD

> 'Hear, O Israel, the Lord is our God, the Lord is One.' (Deuteronomy 6:4)

This is the first sentence of the **Shema** (rhymes with 'bazaar'). It is a prayer that Jews recite every morning and evening (see page 86). It states the basic teaching of Judaism – belief in one God (monotheism). In ancient times people believed that every natural event was controlled by a different god. Today many people believe in one God.

Belief in one God affects how we think about the world and all that is in it. As monotheists, Jews believe that people, trees, flowers, rocks and the rest of nature are all created by the one God. This means that whatever humans see, hear or experience brings them in touch with God.

GOD AS CREATOR

> 'In the beginning, God created heaven and earth.' (Genesis 1:1)

'I see your heavens, the work of your hands; the moon and stars which you have placed there.' (Psalm 8:4)

Jews believe that God created the universe out of nothing. By creating the world out of nothing, God was able to choose exactly how He wanted the world to be. He did not have to rely on using raw materials that might be faulty.

This may be difficult to understand, but think about it like this. Imagine you had the power to turn your thoughts into reality. Your thoughts would then become a creative force or power. You might 'think' a donkey – and suddenly there is a real donkey. Other people can see it, hear it and ride on it. It would be real in every way. However, if you stop thinking about it, it ceases to exist. It only exists as long as your thoughts keep pouring into it.

This is how Jews think of creation. The world is real, but it only exists while God is pouring His creative energies into it. In this way creation is not just a one-off event, it is continuous. This is why Jews praise God who 'in His goodness renews the work of creation each day, continually'.

OMNIPOTENCE, OMNISCIENCE AND OMNIPRESENCE

Jews believe that God is:

- omnipotent – all powerful
- omniscient – knows everything
- omnipresent – exists everywhere.

However, although God is so powerful, Jews believe that He holds back His power and allows people to choose whether they will do good or evil (see page 20). An ancient Jewish teaching says, 'Wherever you find God's greatness, there you will find His humility.' Sometimes God uses His power to step in. Jews call these interventions 'miracles'.

God's knowledge is different from human knowledge. Our knowledge of things around us comes from the way our brains interpret the messages our senses receive. An ancient

Jewish teaching says, 'by knowing Himself He knows all things'. This means that God knows what He has created, what He can create and what He intends to create. God is constantly pouring His creative energy into the things He has created. By knowing Himself, He knows what His power has brought about, i.e. all of creation.

Jews also believe God is omnipresent. He fills the whole universe with His presence. God does not just exist in the spaces left by the solid objects, He is in the solid objects, too. In the same way our thoughts exist within our brain but our thoughts are not solid objects. God is not a physical object, and He remains unchanged after creation. A Jewish prayer says of God, 'You are as You were before the world was created; You are as You are after it is created'.

CONCERN FOR HUMANITY

Jews believe that God is very different from human beings. They believe that God is holy, good, merciful and just – and He expects people to try to be the same, as far as they can be. 'You must be holy because I, the Lord your God, am holy' (*Leviticus 19:2*). Jews believe that people can turn to God in prayer, and that He hears their prayer – but He may not answer in the way people expect.

ADDRESSING GOD

In prayer, Jews speak to God as 'You'. This is because they believe that everyone can have a personal relationship with Him. They may call Him by any of the names He is called in the **Torah**. However, out of respect, they only speak God's names in worship. One name is never pronounced at all. Jews often refer to God as 'Hashem', a word that means 'the name'. This means 'the One whose name we treat with respect and do not pronounce unnecessarily'. In prayer, Jews may also refer to God as father, king, helper, healer, protector, sustainer or similar names.

FACTFILE

The six days of Creation

According to the Bible, God created everything in six days:

At first there was nothing.

Then, God created –

- on the First Day: light and dark, day and night

- on the Second Day: heaven, the sky and water

- on the Third Day: dry land and sea, all kinds of green plants

- on the Fourth Day: stars, sun and moon, seasons and time

- on the Fifth Day: birds, fish and sea monsters

- on the Sixth Day: animals, insects and – finally – human beings.

Judaism teaches that all humanity belongs to God. He wants everyone to serve Him by living their lives the way He wants. The **Noachide Laws** contain the guidelines for this way of life. These laws were given to Noah after the flood (*Genesis* 9). Jews respect the Noachide Laws as a code for both a moral and a spiritual life.

THE NOACHIDE LAWS

The Noachide Laws have seven principles:

(1) They forbid *idolatry*. Idolatry means worshipping an image. For Jews this means worshipping anything other than God – the sun and moon, mountains, animals, a person or a process (e.g. fire). Idolatry is a terrible insult to the true God.

Jews consider that it is idolatry to try to make an image of God (a picture or statue). Human beings cannot understand or even imagine enough about God to make a true image. Therefore images can only show a limited idea of God. This would prevent real worship of the true God.

(2) They forbid *blasphemy*, or cursing God. Judaism expects people to have a respectful and sensitive attitude towards God and spiritual matters.

The Noachide Laws also forbid **(3)** murder, **(4)** theft, **(5)** sexual misconduct (including adultery, incest, homosexuality and sexual relations with animals), and **(6)** cruelty to animals.

Finally the laws demand **(7)** justice. A system of laws with courts to enforce them ensures that people live together in harmony. Setting up a legal system is obeying God's will, as it leads to **tikkun olam**, the improvement of the world.

These seven principles are not a total code of practice. They are a basis upon which a person can build a good life. Judaism teaches that it is the duty of all people, not just Jews, to observe these principles. Jews believe that anyone who breaks these rules cannot be called a civilized human being.

FREEDOM OF CHOICE

> 'I have set before you today life and death, the blessing and the curse; therefore choose life.'
>
> (Deuteronomy 30:19)

The first chapter of the **Torah** (see page 26) tells how God created the first human couple, Adam and Eve. He created them 'in His (i.e. God's) image' (*Genesis 1:27*). Jews take this to mean that, just as God is free to do as He wishes, so every person is free to choose whether to do good or evil. Jews believe that each New Year (see page 44) God decides whether a person will be healthy or sick, clever or dull, rich or poor. However, every person can make moral choices within each situation. Thus each person is responsible for his or her own actions.

The Jewish view of an ideal world – all human beings living under God's Law

OTHER RELIGIONS

Jews believe that non-Jews serve God if they obey the Noachide Laws. They feel that some religions point a way to God. Therefore Jews do not see the need to convert other people to their religion (see page 23).

They recognize that Islam is a monotheistic religion with a strict moral code that upholds the Noachide Laws. This also applies to the Sikh religion.

Jews accept that Christians have high moral principles, but are concerned about the Christian teaching that Jesus is God. They do not think Christians are pure monotheists. Jews are also unhappy about the use of images and icons in Catholic and Orthodox worship. They feel this is rather like idolatry.

However, Jews recognize a special relationship with Christianity and Islam. A twelfth-century scholar described Judaism as the seed of the tree, with Christianity and Islam as the branches.

Many Hindus live by strict moral codes, but others have moral principles with which Judaism would never agree. Also, although Hindus claim to believe in one god, this does not seem to be carried out in practice. They also have many images. Jews respect the moral code of Buddhism but Buddhists do not believe in a god, and they use statues of Buddha in worship.

Jews hope for a time when everyone will serve God. In the **Aleinu** prayer they ask:

> '…may all the inhabitants of the world…bow and prostrate themselves and give honour to the glory of Your Name and accept upon themselves the yoke of Your Kingship…'

FACTFILE

The story of Noah

The story of Noah is really about sin and forgiveness, and God's covenant.

Noah was a good man who 'walked with God' at a time when people were very wicked indeed. God told Noah to build a huge boat, called the Ark, and gave him instructions as to its size and the type of wood to use. Then He told Noah to fill it with a pair of each type of living thing. Noah obeyed Him.

Then the rains came and the world was completely flooded. Only Noah and his family, and the animals in the Ark, survived. The flood lasted a long time.

Eventually, the water subsided, and Noah could let out the animals once more. He praised God. Then God said, 'I establish my covenant with you,' and as a sign of that covenant He placed a rainbow in the sky. Through Noah, God gave human beings another chance.

POINTS OF VIEW

It is difficult for people from different religious groups to live in a multi-ethnic society. Members of one group might disapprove strongly of the teachings of another religion, and some people might want to convert others to their own belief. However, we must strive for peace in our society and avoid conflict.

THE CHOSEN PEOPLE

'You belong to the Lord your God; He has chosen you to be his own people from among all the peoples who live on earth.'

(Deuteronomy 14:2)

The Jews are sometimes called the Chosen People. This does not mean that God has favourites. Rather, the Jews are chosen for a task, not for privilege. Jews believe that all people should serve God by keeping the **Noachide Laws** (see page 20). But the task for which Jews are chosen is to serve God by keeping the 613 commandments (see below).

THE COVENANT

'Today you are standing in the presence of the Lord your God…to enter into the covenant that the Lord your God is making with you…so that the Lord may confirm you as his people and be your God, as he promised you.'

(Deuteronomy 29:10–13)

A covenant is an arrangement where two or more parties agree to look after each other's interests so that they all benefit. Treaties or trade agreements between countries are examples of covenants. Jews understand their relationship with God to be a covenant.

When everyone keeps to the terms of a covenant, each one's needs can be satisfied. God does not exactly have 'needs', but He does have desires. He desires human beings to keep His commandments. By doing this they bring holiness into the world and prepare for the time when all human beings will know Him (*Jeremiah 31:31–4*).

Jews believe that God's part of the covenant relationship is that He will never abandon the Jewish people.

The Bible describes how God made a covenant with Abraham. Later the Israelites entered into a covenant with God and were given the rules by which they were expected to live (*Exodus 19–20*). The first five books of the Bible (the Five Books of Moses) contain the basic rules that God wants the Jews to keep. These books are the **Torah** and are the Jews' most precious possession.

THE MITZVOT (COMMANDMENTS)

'And now Israel, what does the Lord your God expect of you?…to keep, for your own good, the commandments of the Lord…'

(Deuteronomy 10:12–13)

(Israel is another name for the Jewish people.)

Mitzvah (plural mitzvot) means 'commandment'. For Jews, these are the rules that God wants them to keep. There are 613 mitzvot. There are 248 positive rules, the things they are commanded to do, and 365 negative commandments, those things they must not do. The Ten Commandments (see page 26) are part of the 613, and so are the seven principles of the Noachide Laws (see page 20).

Mitzvot as a discipline

Mitzvot are not only about religious observance such as praying or keeping festivals. Mitzvot also include the right way to conduct industrial relations, trials, divorce proceedings, and the food Jews may or may not eat. Keeping the mitzvot means leading a disciplined life.

Mitzvot and ethics

Keeping the commandments helps to build up personal character and establish a fair and just society. For example, the laws about the punishment of criminals (*Deuteronomy 21:22–3*) teach about respect for human dignity. Rules about compensation stress personal responsibility (*Exodus 22:28–23:5*) and the laws about lending teach kindness towards the poor (*Deuteronomy 15:7–11*).

One class of commandment, the **chukim** (statutes) are there to test a Jew's faith. The commandments about eating **kosher** food (see page 68) are chukim.

Mitzvot as connecting with God

Jews understand the mitzvot as God's way of reaching out to people. Observing them is humanity's way of reaching towards God. It is a way of connecting with God.

BECOMING JEWISH

Jews do not try to convert other people to their religion (see page 20). However, some people may decide they wish to become Jewish and there is a procedure for them to do so.

A Jewish court, called **bet din** (see page 97), can carry out conversions. The **dayanim** (judges) lead a person to through a course of instruction in Judaism and teach them to start living as a Jew. They will only finalize the conversion if they are convinced of the person's sincerity.

The convert must formally accept all the mitzvot. This acceptance is essential because a conversion cannot be cancelled. Male converts must be circumcised (see page 72), which is usually done by a Jewish doctor in hospital. Finally the convert is immersed in a **mikveh**, a special pool (see page 82). After rising from the water the convert is fully Jewish and will remain so for life.

THE LAND OF ISRAEL

'And the Lord appeared to Abram and said, "To your descendants I give this land."'

(Genesis 12:7)

To Jews, Israel means both the land that God promised to their ancestors and the modern State of Israel.

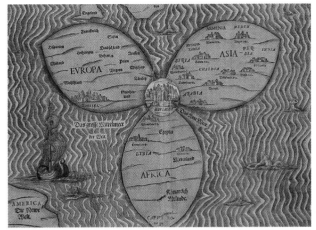

Medieval map showing Jerusalem as the centre of the world

For Jews, Israel is the Holy Land and Jerusalem is the Holy City. Many of the 613 mitzvot can only be kept in Israel. Jerusalem is the centre of the world, from a spiritual point of view. Jews look forward to a time when they will return to Jerusalem and rebuild the Temple. All nations will go there to worship God (*Isaiah 56:7; 66:23*). They believe this will happen when the Messiah comes (see page 24).

FACTFILE

Jerusalem

The city of Jerusalem has existed since 2000 BCE.

When the Israelites entered the Holy Land, the city was a fortress called Jebus and was occupied by the Jebusites.

King David decided to make this his capital city. It was called **Zion**, from the name of the hill on which it stood.

Now it is a holy city for Jews, Christians and Muslims.

THE MESSIAH

'"Behold, days are coming," says the Lord, "…when no person will need to teach another…saying "Know the Lord", for they will all know Me…"'

(Jeremiah 31:31–9)

The word Messiah comes from the Hebrew word **Mashiach** which means 'anointed one'. To anoint a person means to pour holy oil over their head. In ancient times, kings of Israel, prophets and priests were anointed when they were chosen.

The prophets wrote that one day there would be a Messiah who would lead the Jewish people. When the Messiah comes, there would be great changes in the world. The Messiah would bring peace. Animals and human beings would no longer harm one another. Everyone would feel God's presence. Jews therefore think that the present time is just temporary. History – human life as we know it – would one day come to an end and make way for a new spiritual world.

The Messiah would be human, not a god-like being. He would be a descendant of King David. He would be a very holy, learned man and a great leader. Although people have tried to work out when the Messiah will come, no one really knows. Some men have falsely claimed to be the Messiah. Jews still wait and pray for the true Messiah to come.

LIFE AFTER DEATH

'In this world people…do not know the value of what they have brought about. In the world to come they will realize what they have achieved.'

(Midrash)

Jews believe that the period before birth, life in this world, and existence after leaving it are stages in a continual process. People are given a life and guidelines on how they should live it. Jews are expected to be workers for God (see page 22). During life, there will be times when people will be taken off and assessed or judged as to how they are performing. They will not know when this happens. They will be rewarded or punished according to their performance.

REWARD AND PUNISHMENT

Judaism teaches that a person's soul continues after death. When they leave this world they will be rewarded or punished for what they have done in life. The reward is to be close to God. The **Midrash** says, 'The righteous bask in the rays of God's presence.'

Punishment does not mean being sent to hell as a place of everlasting torments. Rather, hell is like a laundry for souls. Jews believe that a person can be cleansed of their sins, even very serious ones, and eventually go to be close to God.

A story in the **Talmud** tells of a righteous man who lost his faith and began to commit sins. After he died the heavenly judges could not decide whether to punish him for his sins, or reward him for his righteousness. It was decided that he should go through the cleansing of hell, so that he could eventually come close to God.

RESURRECTION

Jews believe that one day the dead will rise (be resurrected) and their souls will be reunited with their bodies. This is why Jews do not allow cremation.

THE AUTHORITY OF THE RABBIS

Jews have two sets of teachings. One is the *written* **Torah** (see Unit 12). This is fixed and will not change. Jews believe it to be the word of God. There is also the *oral* Torah, the **halakhah** (see Units 14–15). This is a set of

Learning the importance of the Torah begins at an early age

laws and teachings that interpret the written Torah, to guide Jews in their daily living.

The people responsible for halakhah were originally priests (cohanim) and judges. The priests were descendants of Aaron, Moses' brother, of the tribe of Levi. Judges were scholars but not necessarily priests. They worked together to interpret the Torah, the Jewish Bible.

The authority of the priests and judges to carry out this task is laid down in the written Torah:

'If there is a problem that is too difficult for you…you shall go to the priest, the Levite, or to the judge who will…give you the ruling. You must do according to the ruling he instructs you…'

(Deuteronomy 17:8–11)

Later, mainly the judges interpreted the Torah and the term **rabbi** (teacher or master) came into use.

◇

QUOTE

'As I live, says the LORD God, I have no pleasure in the death of the wicked, but that the wicked turn from his way and live.'

(Ezekeiel 33:11)

FACTFILE

Priests and sacrifices

A priest is a person born to a priestly family. In the Temple the priests used to offer sacrifices of a clean animal or bird. Generally only the best animals could be sacrificed for God.

After the destruction of the Temple in the first century CE, no more sacrifices could be offered, and therefore the role of priest became redundant.

12 THE TORAH

'Moses received the Torah from Sinai, he gave it to Joshua, Joshua gave it to the Elders, the Elders to the Prophets, and the Prophets to the men of the Great Assembly.'

(Ethics of the Fathers)

Torah means 'instruction'. Jews use the word Torah in several ways. It can mean:

- the first five books of the Bible
- the whole of the Bible (the written Torah)
- the whole body of teachings that explain the Bible (the oral Torah).

THE WRITTEN TORAH

The written Torah has three parts:

- Torah (the Five Books of Moses)
- **Nevi'im** (the Books of the Prophets)
- **Ketuvim** (holy writings).

The initial letters of the three parts, (T, N, K) form the word **Tenakh**. This is what Jews call the Bible. The Tenakh is written mainly in Hebrew. Some portions are written in Aramaic, a language similar to Hebrew.

THE TEN COMMANDMENTS

When the Israelites reached Mount Sinai after leaving Egypt there was a great display of God's power, in thunder and lightning. Moses went up the mountain and disappeared in the thick cloud that covered the peak. He returned forty days later. He was carrying two blocks of stone with writing cut into them. These were the Ten Commandments.

While he was on the mountain, Moses learned all that God wanted him to teach the Israelites. There are 613 commandments in all, including those cut in the blocks of stone.

Jews think the Ten Commandments must be kept by *every* Jew, male and female, young and old, everywhere and at all times. Each Commandment can be used as a heading,

The Ten Commandments

1 Know that I am the Lord your God, who brought you out of slavery in Egypt.
2 Worship no god but Me.
3 Do not use my name for evil purposes.
4 Remember to keep the Sabbath day holy; on it do not do any work.
5 Respect your father and your mother.
6 Do not commit murder.
7 Do not commit adultery.
8 Do not steal.
9 Do not accuse anyone falsely.
10 Do not desire a man's house, his wife, nor anything that belongs to him.

(Exodus 20:1–14)

with other commandments listed under it. For example, the command not to steal means that taking someone else's property is wrong. All the rules about injury and compensation, loans and inheritance, come from this basic idea.

TORAH

The first part of the Tenakh, the Five Books of Moses, contain the commandments and the ethical standards of the Jewish people. Below are some notes about the contents of the Five Books.

For Jews these five books are the holiest part of the Tenakh. The Torah's accounts of the

1 *Genesis* (**Bereshit**)
God creates the world; people turn wicked and God sends a flood to destroy them. Noah and his family are saved. Stories of the Patriarchs: Abraham, Isaac and Jacob. Jacob's sons settle in Egypt (see page 6).

2 *Exodus* (**Shemot**)
Jacob's descendants become slaves in Egypt. Moses leads the Israelites to

freedom. They cross the Reed Sea (not Red Sea). They receive the Torah (see page 52) and build a sanctuary, a portable temple (see page 7).

3 *Leviticus* (**Vayikra**)
How sacrifices were offered. Foods Jews may or may not eat (see page 68). Major festivals and **mitzvot** that must be observed.

4 *Numbers* (**Bemidbar**)
Moses counts the Israelites. Some rebel against him. The Israelites' victories. The Israelites' route from Egypt to the Promised Land.

5 *Deuteronomy* (**Devarim**)
Also called **Mishnah Torah**, 'repeating the Torah'. Speeches by Moses on the borders of the Promised Land, laws and ethical teachings. The death of Moses.

patriarchs and matriarchs, slavery in Egypt and the journey to the Promised Land tell Jews who they are. The laws and moral teachings tell Jews how to live and fulfil God's will.

The Torah is the source of strength and inspiration for Jews. They have faithfully copied the words onto parchment scrolls. They have studied and thought about the Torah and tried to understand its meaning. They have lived by the laws of the Torah, and have been prepared to die for them.

Throughout history, wherever there have been Jews there have been copies of the Torah, their most precious possession. Children learn about the Torah from an early age, and parents want them to live by their teachings. At home, Jews have the Torah in a printed book form called a **chumash**.

Torah scrolls in their cases

FACTFILE

Moses

Having led the Israelites out of Egypt and throughout their wanderings in the wilderness, Moses died before they entered the Holy Land.

'Moses, the servant of the Lord died there in the land of Moab…Moses was a hundred and twenty years old when he died; his eye was not dim nor his natural force abated. And the people of Israel wept for Moses.

…And there has not arisen a prophet since in Israel like Moses, whom the Lord knew face to face, none like him for all the signs and the wonders which the Lord sent him to do in the land of Egypt…and for all the mighty power and all the great deeds which Moses did in the sight of all Israel.'

(Deuteronomy 34:5–12)

13 THE TENAKH

Jews regard the Five Books of Moses as the most holy part of the **Tenakh**. However, they also regard the **Nevi'im** (prophets) and **Ketuvim** (holy writings) as sacred. This is because they were written by prophets or other people inspired by God's spirit.

NEVI'IM (BOOKS OF THE PROPHETS)

The books of *Joshua*, *Judges*, *Samuel* and *Kings* describe the history of the Israelites from the death of Moses. They tell of the Israelites' battles to conquer their new land and how they fought off hostile neighbours. They describe how they set up a monarchy and the building of the Temple. Then the land was divided into two kingdoms (Israel and Judah). There is the account of the exile of the people of Israel to Assyria, followed by the destruction of the Temple and the exile of the Jews to Babylon.

The history is actually a teaching on religion. It shows how the covenant (see page 22) works out in the history of the Jewish people.

The other books in this section are the three long books of *Isaiah*, *Jeremiah* and *Ezekiel*, and the twelve short books known simply as 'the twelve'. Isaiah lived during the Assyrian invasion and the exile of the Northern Kingdom of Israel (see page 7). Jeremiah and Ezekiel both foretold the destruction of Jerusalem. Ezekiel was taken into exile in Babylon and told his prophecy to the Jews there. Jeremiah actually saw the destruction of the Temple. There is not much history in these books as their purpose is to teach faith, justice and compassion.

KETUVIM (HOLY WRITINGS)

The books in this section are of several kinds. *Esther*, *Daniel*, *Ezra* and *Nehemiah* describe events in the Persian period (see page 8). *Chronicles* is a history of the Jews. Again, the purpose of these books is to show how the

Jews behaved towards God and how this affected their history.

The book of *Psalms* is a collection of 150 songs and poems of praise to God. Most were written by David. *Proverbs* consists of short sayings giving advice for right living.

Job is the story of a righteous man whom God tested by making him suffer. Job's friends tell him he must have sinned to deserve this torment, but he insists he has not. Job accepts his suffering and concludes that no one can understand the workings of God's mind. One of the main points of the book is that suffering is not necessarily due to sin (see page 102).

Ecclesiastes is about the meaning of life. It looks at human limitations and compares them with the immense power of God. It concludes, 'The end of the matter is,...fear God and keep His commandments, for this is the whole of man.'

Ruth was a Moabite woman who lived at the time of the judges (see page 7). She loved God and endured poverty and hardship to join the Jewish people. David was her great-grandson. Jews expect the Messiah (see page 24) to be her descendant.

In the sad book of *Lamentations*, Jeremiah describes the destruction of Jerusalem and the Temple. He had been warning the Jews of this for years. It is a book full of tragedy and anguish, expressed in poetry.

The *Song of Songs* tells of the love of God and the Jewish people for one another. It is expressed as a love poem in which a shepherdess seeks her shepherd lover. It contains some of the most beautiful verses in the Tenakh.

USES OF THE NEVI'IM AND KETUVIM

Parts of the Nevi'im and Ketuvim are used in worship. The *Psalms* are part of daily and weekly prayers. Some are used for special

Reading the Megillah (scroll of Esther) on Purim

occasions. For example, Psalms 121 and 130 are often said before praying for a sick person. Extracts from the Nevi'im are read in the synagogue after the **Torah** readings.

Song of Songs, *Ruth*, *Ecclesiastes*, *Esther* and *Lamentations* are known as the **Chamesh Megillot** (the Five Scrolls). They are read in the synagogue on festival days (see pages 48–61).

The book of *Jonah* is read on **Yom Kippur** (Day of Atonement, see page 46). This is the day when Jews pray for their sins to be forgiven. It tells of a prophet called Jonah, whom God sent to clean up the wicked city of Nineveh. When the people hear that God will destroy them they are shocked and become aware of their sinfulness. They sincerely repent and God forgives them.

◇

FACTFILE 1

King David

David had a varied career: shepherd, song-writer, warrior and king.

FACTFILE 2

Psalm 119

This is the longest Psalm. It has twenty-two stanzas (parts). Each stanza is made up of eight couplets. It is written in alphabetical sequence. Each line in the first stanza begins with *alef* (the first letter of the Hebrew alphabet, or *alefbet*). The lines of the second stanza begin with *bet* (the second letter of the alefbet) and the third stanza's lines begin with *gimel*, and so on.

HALAKHAH – JEWISH LAW

Halakhah (plural halakhot) really means 'going'. Jews think of following the commandments as 'going with God'.

The 613 **mitzvot** (see page 22) in the written **Torah** are stated briefly. For example, *Deuteronomy* 6:8 says, 'bind a sign on your arms', but it does not say what the sign is. According to tradition, God gave Moses the Torah and also taught him the halakhot – how the commandments were to be kept.

For centuries the halakhot were passed down by word of mouth. Sometimes people wanted more explanation of halakhot. For example, the Torah said a Moabite could not join the Jewish people. They wanted to know if this applied to a Moabitess.

NEW SITUATIONS

In new situations the Jews needed to know how to apply the laws. For example, did crops from newly conquered territories have to be tithed (a portion given to the priests)? The Jews in exile wanted to know how to conduct worship when they didn't have a Temple. At first these questions were settled by priests and judges (*Deuteronomy* 17:8–11) and later by **rabbis** (see page 25). Later still these rulings were given authority by the supreme court Judges, later called the **Sanhedrin**. These rulings were also passed on orally. Hence the halakhah became known as the oral Torah.

'PUTTING A FENCE ROUND THE TORAH'

Judges and, later, rabbis made extra rules to help people not to disobey the Torah. For example, the Torah forbids lighting a fire on **Shabbat**. The rabbis forbade handling flint or other fire-making equipment so people would not make a fire accidentally. This is called 'putting a fence round the Torah'.

CLASSIFYING THE HALAKHAH

By the end of the first century BCE there was a vast number of rulings. The rabbis wanted a system. **Hillel** the Elder set down seven principles as guidelines for making halakhic rulings. Rabbi Akiva (d. 135 CE) began to classify the halakhot under headings. He wanted to show how they related to the written Torah. Rabbi Meir, a pupil of Rabbi Akiva, continued this work. Until this time, halakhah were still taught orally, though teachers made notes to remind themselves.

THE MISHNAH

Roman rule forced Jews to leave the Holy Land during the second century CE. The Jews feared that they would lose contact with their religious roots. The leading rabbi, Judah the Prince, decided it was time to write down the oral Torah. This was so that Jews all over the world would have a book with the most important halakhot to refer to. This became the **Mishnah**. It has 63 volumes, or tractates, in six divisions. These are the topics covered.

1. **Zeraim** (seeds) Prayer, crops that were to be left for the poor, giving tithes, Shemitta (a year when no farm work was to be done).

2. **Moed** (festivals) How Sabbaths and festivals are to be observed, sacrifices in the Temple, forbidden types of work, fasts and other special days, mourning.

3. **Nashim** (women) Betrothal and marriage, marriage documents, people forbidden to marry, divorce and settlements, vows.

4. **Nezikin** (damages) Injury and compensation, ownership, inheritance, court procedures, examining witnesses, punishments a court could

impose. One volume called *Ethics* or *Sayings of the Fathers*, deals with morals (see page 33).

5. **Kedoshim** (holy matters) Deals with the different kinds of sacrifices offered in the Temple, sacrifices that were unfit for offering, the layout of the Temple.

6. **Taharot** (purities) How people or things could become pure or impure (see page 82), the **mikveh** (immersion pool), food laws.

A later collection called the **Tosefta** (addition) contains material not included in the Mishnah.

A page of Talmud. The text of the Talmud is in the middle. On the right is Rashi's commentary; the Tosafot are on the left.

THE TALMUD

Rabbis and students began to study the Mishnah in Israel and Babylon from the end of the second century CE. They wanted to know how the halakhot had been decided and what they meant for the Jews of their day. Their discussions were written down and filed away. In about 500 CE Rabbi Ina and Rabbi Ashi of Babylon put these records in order. They wrote down each paragraph of the Mishnah. Round this they wrote the discussions that had taken place. Some of these rulings went back centuries to the oral tradition. The result was first the Jerusalem Talmud, and then the Babylonian Talmud (Talmud Bavli) – a massive work. The Bavli is studied more widely and is known simply as the Talmud. Jews also call it **gemara**, meaning 'learning'. Today Talmud is the main subject studied in **yeshivot**, Jewish academies (see page 89).

COMMENTARIES

The best commentary to guide people through the Talmud is the one written by **Rashi** (Rabbi Shlomo ben Yitzhak, 1040–1105, see page 9). After Rashi there were more **Tosafot** additions. These analyse particular points in a discussion or compare them with other discussions. On the left is a page of a printed Talmud.

FACTFILE

Rashi (1040–1105 CE)

Rashi's great commentary on the Bible and Talmud is still studied by almost every student in yeshivot. His commentary on the Bible was the first printed Hebrew book, and was issued in 1475. Rashi lived in France and earned his living as a wine merchant.

The **Talmud** includes the discussions of learned men over several centuries. It is not organized in a systematic way. For example, a discussion about Passover may refer to the Sabbath as a comparison. A discussion about mourning may also refer to mourning on the Sabbath. So discussions about Sabbath observance may be scattered throughout the Talmud. **Rabbis** had to have a very good knowledge of the whole Talmud to be able to locate particular topics. This was difficult because the Talmud is huge. Studying it at a page a day would take fourteen years to complete. Also, it needs to be updated continually to take account of other halakhic decisions. Two methods emerged for dealing with this: *responsa* and *codes*.

RESPONSA

From about the seventh century, a few very learned rabbis were consulted by other rabbis on difficult questions. The most famous rabbis were the **gaonim** (see page 8), heads of the Babylonian academies. The gaonim would send replies (*responsa*) to rabbis in different countries. Later these *responsa* were collected and published. Rabbis could use them to work out answers to new problems.

CODES

The Codes of Jewish Law are a collection of **halakhah** set down in order. The two most important were:

- the **Mishnah Torah** of Rabbi Moses ben Maimon (Maimonides, 1135–1204) where the halakhot are set down under separate headings
- The **Shulchan Aruch** (table prepared) of Rabbi Yosef Caro (1488–1575). This omitted all laws that no longer applied in Judaism (e.g. rules concerning the Temple), and set everything else in clear, short paragraphs. The Shulchan Aruch became the model for modern Jewish law.

Keeping Judaism in an age of advancing technology

HALAKHAH AS AN ONGOING PROCESS

Conditions change, bringing new discoveries, new ways of living and new social attitudes. Jews need new decisions to enable them to keep their part of the covenant with God (see page 22).

Technology presents its own problems for Jews. For example, is it all right to use automatic switches on the Sabbath? Is computer hacking theft? Is a person on a life-support machine alive or dead?

To enable rabbis to answer these questions, the Shulchan Aruch has been updated with new additions. Whole books are published dealing with particular topics. Some rabbis specialize in particular areas of halakhah. The continual discussion and refining of halakhah is an ongoing process.

AGADAH (TEACHING THE MEANING OF THE TENAKH)

Agadah (telling) is the traditional way of explaining the verses of the Bible. Each word is carefully studied and compared with similar words in other verses. It was originally passed on orally, like the halakhah. Later, people began to write down the agadah. These writings were called **Midrashim**. The writers often used parables or examples from real life to explain what they said. Many of them were included in the Talmud.

KABBALAH (MYSTICISM)

Kabbalah means 'that which is received'. It is the study of the secrets of the **Torah**. Kabbalistic writings explain the ways in which God reveals Himself and the nature of His relationship with human beings. It discusses the character of the human soul and how evil can exist in a world created by a good God.

Jews did not examine these topics just to gain knowledge. They studied kabbalah to understand their relationship with God better. By doing this, they could serve God with greater devotion.

Kabbalah have been studied from the early days of Judaism. However, they were written down gradually over hundreds of years. The **Zohar** (*Book of Splendour*) is the most important kabbalistic writing. It was published in the fourteenth century.

In the eighteenth century Rabbi Israel Baal Shem Tov enabled more people to study Kabbalah by explaining it in a simpler way.

ETHICAL WRITINGS

Jews study the Bible, Talmud and midrashim because it can lead to good deeds. An old saying is, 'Anyone whose good deeds are more than his wisdom, his wisdom will endure. Anyone whose wisdom is more than his good deeds, his wisdom will not endure.'

There has always been Jewish literature about developing good character and good behaviour. The oldest is the book of *Proverbs* in the Bible (see page 28). In the **Mishnah** the *Ethics of the Fathers* deals solely with moral guidance (see page 31). These and later ethical works became important in the **Musar movement** (see page 128).

FACTFILE

Jewish ethics

Jewish ethics (teachings about morals) are based on the Biblical idea that mankind is created in God's image and must strive to live according to God's will. This includes loving one's neighbour as oneself. The great Rabbi **Hillel** said, 'What is hateful to you, do not [do it] unto your fellow-man.'

FACTFILE 2

Some Kabbalistic ideas

Kabbalah is Jewish mysticism. Early Kabbalists thought of divinity as a pure, infinite, spiritual light whose rays account for all creation. They believed that the human soul was formed in the 'upper spheres' and that the goal of the soul is to come closer to God. They believed Jews should live in a state of holiness, fellowship and unity.

'These are the festivals of the Lord, holy assemblies which you shall proclaim at their appointed times.'

(Leviticus 23:4)

There are many Jewish festivals during the year. Some of these involve Jews in prayer and celebration with their families. On these days there is no work, school or shopping to be done. Other, less important, celebrations do not affect daily life so much. They may simply need special prayers to be said.

HISTORICAL COMMEMORATIONS

Festivals such as **Pesach** (see page 48) and **Hanukkah** (see page 56) commemorate (remember) historical events. They remember the way that God created miracles to help the Jewish people. On these days Jews praise God as the One who controls human history. When Jews observe these festivals they try to recreate or re-enact the original event. This involves special **mitzvot**.

CELEBRATING GOD'S CREATION

Holy days such as **Shabbat** (Sabbath, see page 36) and the New Year for Trees (see page 62) focus on God as the One who creates and controls nature.

Pesach, **Shavuot** and **Sukkot** celebrate both historical events and nature. Pesach and Shavuot are harvest festivals, and Sukkot marks the beginning of the rainy season in the Holy Land.

YOM KIPPUR AND SIMCHAT TORAH

Two festivals do not link up with history or natural events. **Yom Kippur**, the Day of Atonement, is about re-establishing the relationship with God and with other human beings. **Simchat Torah** celebrates the ending of the cycle of readings from the **Torah** and the beginning of the new cycle.

The chart opposite shows how the festivals can be classified under these headings.

THE JEWISH CALENDAR

Jews use the Biblical method of counting time. Each new day starts at sunset. For example, when the sun goes down on Friday evening, it will be Saturday for Jews. This is why Sabbath, which occurs on Saturday, actually begins on Friday evening. All Jewish festivals start at sunset. As times of sunset change with the seasons, Jews have to change the times when they begin festivals, such as Shabbat.

The chart opposite shows how the Jewish year (**Tishrei** to **Ellul**) compares with the year January to December.

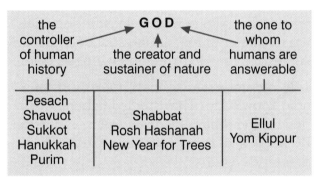

The festivals mark different aspects of a Jew's relationship with God

FACTFILE

Busy and not-so-busy

Looking at the chart opposite, you will notice that some months are much busier than others. **Tishrei** has seven major Jewish festivals and **Iyar** has four.

Cheshvan has no celebrations at all! For this reason it is also known as Marcheshvan – or 'bitter Cheshvan' – because there is nothing to celebrate.

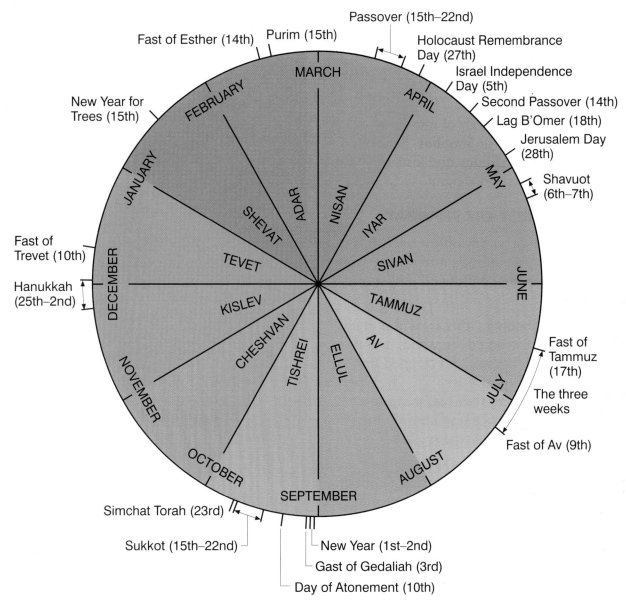

The Jewish year

'God said to Moses "I have a precious gift in My treasure house, 'Sabbath' is its name. Go and tell the people of Israel that I wish to give it to them."'

(Talmud)

Sabbath is the weekly day of rest for Jews. They call it **Shabbat** or **Shabbos**. Shabbat begins at sunset on Friday and lasts until the stars appear on Saturday night.

WHY JEWS REST ON SHABBAT

Shabbat is not just a day off for Jews, it is a holy day. Jews are not meant to do any work so that they can concentrate on prayer and **Torah** study.

By resting on Shabbat, Jews show that they believe that God created the world, and that after completing His work he stopped and created nothing new (*Genesis 2:1–3*). When they rest on Shabbat, they are, in a way, imitating God. They are also obeying the fourth Commandment (*Exodus 20:8–11*, see page 26).

This modern world is very stressful. Shabbat is an opportunity for the family to spend a relaxing day together.

PREPARING FOR SHABBAT

Jewish families like to make sure that on Shabbat the atmosphere in the home is different from the rest of the week. As no work must be done on Shabbat, they must get ready in advance. Most of the shopping and preparation is left until Friday. To see what happens, we are going to follow the Greens as they celebrate Shabbat.

SHABBAT WITH A JEWISH FAMILY

The Green family think of Shabbat as a special guest who comes to visit each week. Friday afternoon is very busy as there is a lot to do to get ready. In winter, when it gets dark early, Mrs Green leaves work at lunchtime

Friday afternoon; the Green children prepare for Shabbat

and Mr Green returns home early from the office to prepare for Shabbat. Naomi (aged 20), Aaron (aged 16) and Miriam (aged 8) help to clean and tidy the house.

Naomi and Aaron have lots of friends who constantly phone them. On Shabbat, the Greens do not use the phone except in a life-threatening emergency. Nor do they switch on the television. Shabbat is meant to be special – a day of peace and restfulness.

On Shabbat the best cutlery and crockery are used. Candlesticks sparkle on the table, and there is wine and **challot** (Shabbat loaves, see page 40). Sometimes Mrs Green bakes her own challot, or she buys them in a Jewish shop.

Mrs Green prepares all the food in advance. Late on Friday afternoon she places a sheet of metal called a **blech** over the cooker rings. Then she can put the hot cooked food on top, moving the saucepans to cooler or hotter parts of the blech, as necessary. This stops the food from drying out or burning as it is not directly over the flame.

Housework finished, every member of the family has a bath and changes into their Shabbat clothes. As they are not allowed to turn lights on or off on Shabbat, they switch on all the lights they expect to use before

Shabbat begins. Then these lights stay on until Saturday night.

WELCOMING SHABBAT

It is the woman's privilege to welcome the holy day. Mrs Green lights her candles to show Shabbat has begun. As she lights the candles, she beckons with her arms as though to welcome the Shabbat into her home. She covers her eyes and recites the blessing. She says a short prayer for her family. It is a very special, holy moment.

Mrs Green lights her candles

REFLECTIONS

'Lighting Shabbat candles connects me to an endless stream of Jewish mothers through all of time.'

(Mrs R, North London)

'When I light the Shabbat candles I feel like God is blessing me.'

(Mrs M, Glasgow)

Meanwhile, Mr Green takes Aaron to the synagogue. (Sometimes Mrs Green and the girls go too.) At the evening service Shabbat is greeted as a bride coming to meet her husband, the Jewish people. The service ends with the **rabbi** taking a cup of wine and reciting **kiddush** (sanctification, or making holy). This is to thank God for giving Shabbat to the Jewish people.

As they leave the synagogue, they shake hands with their friends and wish each other **'Shabbat Shalom'** or 'a peaceful Shabbat').

THE FRIDAY NIGHT MEAL

Back at home Mr Green blesses his children. He prays that they will grow up to follow the examples of the righteous men and women of Jewish history. Then he recites kiddush.

Every member of the family listens quietly to the blessings and answers, **'Amen'**.

After kiddush they go to wash their hands to make them pure (see page 65). Mr Green blesses the challot and thanks God for 'bringing bread out of the ground'. Jews should thank God before eating any food. Mr Green cuts the bread and dips the pieces in salt (see page 61) before passing them round. The meal begins.

For the Green family, the Shabbat meal is different from any other meal. They eat special food and take time to talk about their week. The parents tell stories to their children. It is a good time to be together.

FACTFILE

Blessings

When Mr Green blesses his children he says to Aaron, 'May God make you as Ephraim and Manasseh.' Then he says to the girls, 'May God make you as Sarah, Rebecca, Rachel and Leah.' Finally he thanks God for his wife who creates a home where God is always present.

SHABBAT MORNING

The synagogue service on **Shabbat** morning (Saturday) begins later and lasts longer than the weekday services.

The **Sefer Torah** (Torah scrolls) are kept in a cupboard, called the Ark. The Ark is opened and everyone stands up as a mark of respect. A Sefer Torah is taken out and carried to the **bimah** (raised platform, see page 84). The **rabbi** reads aloud in Hebrew from the Torah. A portion, called the **sidra**, is read every Sabbath so that the entire scroll is read during the course of a year. Seven men are called to recite blessings at certain points during the reading of the sidra. An eighth man is called to read the **haftarah**, a portion from one of the books of the prophets (see page 29). Then the scrolls are returned to the Ark.

The rabbi then gives a sermon, a talk about the sidra or about an item in the news. He encourages the congregation to keep the faith, or teaches them something new. There follows another service called **musaf** (see page 86).

As people leave the synagogue they again wish each other '**Shabbat Shalom**'.

At home, the midday meal is very like Friday's evening meal. Mr Green does not bless the children again, but he says **kiddush** and recites a blessing over the **challot**. There is more storytelling, which the children enjoy.

After dinner Mr Green sits down with Aaron and Miriam to go over their Jewish studies. Naomi goes out to run a Shabbat playgroup for younger children. Later Miriam may play with friends who live nearby. Mr and Mrs Green may go for a walk, or have a short nap. They do not use their car on Shabbat.

Later in the afternoon, Mr Green and Aaron go to the synagogue for the short afternoon prayers. The Sefer Torah is taken out and the first part of the following week's sidra is read.

Mr Green performs Havdalah. Miriam holds the candle

Mr Green and Aaron study the Torah with the other men until dark. Mrs Green and the girls may go to a women's study group.

SHABBAT GOES OUT

When the stars appear on Saturday night, Shabbat is over. The congregation prays the weekday evening service. They ask God to bless the coming week. Then the rabbi performs **havdalah** (separation). He says a blessing over a cup of wine, and another over spices. He says a third blessing over the light of a candle. There is one last blessing over wine, and the separation of the holy day from the ordinary week is completed.

When Mr Green gets home he also performs havdalah. Then the dishes can be washed!

KEY WORDS

Shabbat/Sabbath – from a Hebrew verb meaning 'to rest' or 'to cease', hence the day of rest for Jews
Sefer Torah – Torah scrolls (*sefer* actually means 'book')
Bimah – raised platform where the Torah is read
Kiddush – 'sanctification', a prayer asking for God's blessing
Challot – enriched, plaited bread eaten at the Shabbat meal
Havdalah – 'separation', a ceremony marking the separation of the Shabbat from the rest of the week

RECIPE

Poppy-seed plait for Shabbat

Ingredients:
450 g strong plain flour
15 g fresh yeast
225 ml tepid water
1 · 5 ml spoon salt
30 ml olive oil
1 egg (beaten)

For the glaze and topping:
beaten egg
poppy seeds

Method:
Lightly grease a baking sheet. Put 150 g of flour into a large bowl. Crumble the yeast into a jug, add the water and stir until dissolved. Add to the flour and mix well. Set this aside in a warm place until frothy – about 20 minutes.

Mix remaining flour with salt and stir in olive oil. Add the egg and the flour mixture to the yeast batter and mix well to give a soft dough. Turn the dough on to a lightly floured surface and knead until smooth and not sticky. Place in a bowl, cover with a lightly oiled plastic sheet and leave to rise. When doubled in size, knead again, then divide the dough in two and roll each half into an oblong. Cut each half into three strips lengthways. Pinch the dough together at the top, then plait the strips. Damp the ends to seal them together. Place on the greased baking sheet. Brush with egg and sprinkle with poppy seeds. Bake at 190°C (gas mark 5) for about 25 minutes.

THE SYMBOLS OF SHABBAT

A symbol is something used to represent something else. In particular, it is a physical object that stands for an idea. Many of the objects used for **Shabbat** are symbolic.

The challot (Sabbath loaves)

When the Israelites made their journey through the wilderness, God gave them manna, miracle food (*Exodus 16:14–18*). On Friday, God gave them a double portion. This was so they would have enough for Shabbat. The two **challot** of the Shabbat meal represent the double portion of manna.

The board under the loaves represents the ground. The embroidered cloth over the loaves represent the dew that covered the manna. The challot are plaited. The twelve plaits represent the twelve loaves of bread set out in the Temple (see page 7) each Shabbat.

Mr Green says a blessing before cutting the challot

The candles

Before electricity, Jews would light lots of candles on Friday evening. This created a festive mood. Today, Jews light two symbolic candles. These represent the Biblical commands, 'Remember the Sabbath day' (*Exodus 20:8*) and 'Observe the Sabbath day' (*Deuteronomy 5:12*). Many families light an extra candle for each child.

Havdalah spices

Many Jews feel more spiritual on Shabbat than on other days. Ancient **rabbis** described this as 'having an extra soul'. When Shabbat ends, the extra soul leaves. The scent of the spices 'refreshes the soul' after the departure of its 'companion'.

Havdalah candles

Jews are not allowed to make fire on Shabbat (*Exodus 35:3*). At **havdalah** they use a plaited candle so that the flames of several wicks mingle. This shows they can now make fire in any form.

WORK FORBIDDEN ON SHABBAT

Just what do Jews mean by 'work' on Shabbat? The rabbi leads the services on Shabbat and earns his living at it. Is this not work? Observant Jews do not turn on light switches, or carry even a handkerchief in their pockets on Shabbat. How can these be considered work?

When Jews talk about 'work' on Shabbat they do not mean following an occupation or using up energy. For the Jew, there are some kinds of work that are called **melachot** (singular melachah). There are 39 melachot that are forbidden on Shabbat. These are the jobs that were needed for building the sanctuary, the portable Temple that the Israelites carried in the desert (see page 7).

These tasks were very varied. It is easier not to describe them as work, but to use the

Hebrew 'melachah'. The 39 forbidden melachot are:

1	ploughing	23	sewing
2	sowing	24	tearing
3	reaping	25	trapping or hunting
4	sheaf-making	26	slaughtering
5	threshing	27	skinning
6	winnowing	28	tanning
7	selecting	29	scraping pelts
8	sifting	30	marking out
9	grinding	31	cutting to shape
10	kneading	32	writing
11	baking	33	erasing
12	sheep-shearing	34	building
13	bleaching	35	demolishing
14	combing raw fibres	36	lighting a fire
15	dyeing	37	putting out a fire
16	spinning	38	the final hammer blow (finishing off a new article)
17 – 19	various weaving operations		
20	separating into threads	39	carrying from a private to a public area and vice versa.
21	tying a knot		
22	untying a knot		

These tasks are forbidden on Shabbat, however they are done. A fire can be lit by rubbing sticks together, or turning a switch. The first method takes a lot of effort, the other takes hardly any. But both create fire, so each is a melachah and is forbidden. This applies to all 39 melachot.

Jews are forbidden to drive on Shabbat, to use the telephone (except for emergencies), watch television, play computer games, take photographs or go fishing. They may go for a walk, or go window-shopping. But they may not take a ball to play, or buy anything. In Israel the buses do not run. Each of these involves doing a melachah.

For observant Jews, Shabbat is a joy that they look forward to all the week. They feel that 'all the days of the week are blessed by Shabbat'.

FACTFILE

Melachot and permitted work

The 39 forbidden melachot are not single jobs, but broad groups of tasks. For example, ploughing means preparing ground for planting and includes digging, fertilizing soil and removing stones. Sewing is joining two materials permanently by means of a third substance. It also includes stapling bits of paper together.

Here are some of the jobs that are not permitted on Shabbat:

- making a bouquet of flowers – this involves reaping and sheaf-making
- filing metals – this involves cutting to shape or finishing off a new article
- shaving – surprisingly, because it is like sheep-shearing
- ironing ('thank-goodness' you say!) – because it is like combing fibres
- putting on make-up – it means putting on colour (dyeing) and marking out
- knitting – separating threads and tying knots
- sealing envelopes, as in sewing – joining two materials by means of another
- squashing a spider – slaughtering
- polishing shoes – tanning or scraping pelts (animal skins).

Permitted work

Anything that is necessary in an emergency is allowed:

- doctors may attend patients
- you may rescue a person from danger or give life-saving help.

For everyday life, Jews use the same calendar as everyone else. But they also have their own calendar (see Unit 16). This follows the phases of the moon (lunar months). **Rosh Chodesh** (new moon) covers two days in some months, depending when the change in the moon's phase occurs.

THE JEWISH MONTHS

The moon takes about 29.5 days to orbit the Earth. During this time its appearance changes as it seems to grow in size and shrink again to nothing. Its reappearance is called the new moon. This is when the new month starts for Jews. These months have 29 or 30 days. There are 12 months in the Jewish year, with an extra month in leap years (see below). All Jewish festivals occur on set dates in this calendar.

The Jewish months do not match up exactly with the January–December calendar. For example, the Jewish New Year is on the first two days of the month of **Tishrei**. This can be any time between early September and early October (see page 35). Jews run their religious life according to the Jewish calendar. They run their businesses or other activities by the general calendar.

ROSH CHODESH IN ANCIENT TIMES

Astronomers in ancient times could work out where and when the new moon would appear. **Torah** law said that people who had seen it must go to the **bet din hagadol**, the supreme Jewish court (see page 30). They had to say the new moon had appeared. Then the **rabbis** would stand up and proclaim, 'It [i.e. the new month] is sanctified, it is sanctified.' Then they sent messengers to tell the Jewish communities they should start counting the new month.

The rabbis also had to make sure that the festivals were celebrated at the right times. The lunar year is about ten days shorter than the solar year which governs the seasons. As lunar years passed, the festivals fell behind the seasons. Within ten years, Passover, a spring festival, would have taken place in midwinter. To overcome this problem, the rabbis put in an extra month. Leap years have thirteen months, and they occur seven times in every nineteen years.

When the second Temple was destroyed (see page 8), the supreme Jewish court came to an end. The rabbis then worked out a permanent calendar. This recurred every nineteen years and is the calendar that Jews use today. The chart on page 35 shows the Jewish months with the January–December calendar.

In ancient Israel, Rosh Chodesh was a day of rest. During the Middle Ages it became a day when women rested. Today, all Jews work on Rosh Chodesh, though in some communities women do not do certain tasks.

THE SABBATH OF BLESSING

The **Shabbat** before Rosh Chodesh is called **Shabbat Mevarchim** (Sabbath of Blessing). After the Torah has been read, everyone in the synagogue stands to hear the declaration of the time of the next new moon, like in the ancient Jewish court. Then the people pray, asking God to bless the coming month as a month of 'life and peace, gladness and joy, deliverance and consolation'.

PRAYERS

The special prayers in the synagogue on Rosh Chodesh include part of **Hallel** (a reading of Psalms 113–118). There are readings from the Torah about sacrifices in the ancient Temple for Rosh Chodesh.

WOMEN'S ROSH CHODESH GROUPS

Today some women meet on Rosh Chodesh to strengthen their Jewish roots.

Women at a North London Rosh Chodesh group listen to a visiting speaker

They have revived some ancient Rosh Chodesh customs. For example, they light a candle floating in water to represent the moon floating in space. Each group manages its own meeting. Some read from the **Tenakh** or other Jewish writings. Some have formal study sessions. Others discuss topics that affect Jewish women. Many have a celebration meal. Most have a charity collection. They all want to deepen their spiritual awareness.

BLESSING OVER THE MOON

During the first half of the month, **Kiddush Levanah** is said on Saturday night after Shabbat. This is a blessing thanking God for renewing the moon. Jews recognize that God keeps order and harmony in the universe.

Once every 28 years Jews recite a blessing over the sun. This is when the Earth and sun are in the same positions, relative to each other, as they were at their creation. Jews recite this blessing to thank God for creating the universe and taking care of it.

FACTFILE

Hallel

Psalms 113–18 contain very beautiful poetry praising God and giving thanks. Here is part of Psalm 118:

Out of my distress I called on the LORD;
the LORD answered and set me free.
With the LORD on my side I do not fear.
What can man do to me?
The LORD is on my side to help me;
I shall look in triumph on those who hate me.
It is better to take refuge in the LORD
than to put any confidence in princes.

'"Seek the Lord while He may be found" (Isaiah 5:6). This refers to the ten days between Rosh Hashanah and Yom Kippur when God is closest to those who sincerely want to return to Him.'

(Talmud)

Rosh Hashanah (New Year) and, ten days later, **Yom Kippur** (Day of Atonement) are called the Days of Awe. Some Jews call them the High Holy Days.

THE DAYS OF AWE

Jews think of Rosh Hashanah as the birthday of the human race. It is the anniversary of the day God created the first human beings (see page 20). On this day Jews believe that God judges people for their actions of the past year and decides their future for the following year. On Rosh Hashanah God decides…

'…how many shall pass away and how many shall be born, who shall live and who shall die…who shall be at peace and who shall be harassed, who shall be poor and who shall be rich…'

(Rosh Hashanah service)

Jews think of Rosh Hashanah as the day when God 'writes down' the decisions. Yom Kippur is the day when they are sealed, or finalized.

THE MONTH OF ELLUL

The **Midrash** says that people can ask God to forgive them at any time. However, for Jews, the month of **Ellul** is a special time for repentance. They remember how, on 1 Ellul, Moses went up Mount Sinai (see page 26) a second time. He went to receive the Ten Commandments carved on stone tablets. These were to replace the ones that were smashed in the incident of the golden calf (see page 27). He returned forty days later, on 10 **Tishrei**, with the new tablets. This showed that God had forgiven the Israelites.

A rabbi shows a class how to blow the shofar

Jews think of this month as a time for putting right the mistakes and misdeeds of the past year. They prepare to renew their relationship with God on a fresh basis.

The Green family take Ellul seriously. Mr Green and Aaron attend the synagogue each morning. The **rabbi** blows the **shofar**, or ram's horn, to remind the congregation that Rosh Hashanah is drawing near. The shofar is a very ancient musical instrument. In olden times its sound signalled troop movements to the armies on the battlefield. It could also signal the approach of the king. At Rosh Hashanah it is blown to remind Jews of their promises to their King (God).

Sephardim (Oriental Jews) rise early during Ellul to say **selichot**, special prayers for forgiveness. **Ashkenazim** (western Jews) say selichot only in the last part of the month.

In the days leading up to Rosh Hashanah the Green family sends cards to their friends wishing them a 'Happy New Year'.

THE EVE OF ROSH HASHANAH

On the last day of the old year Mr Green and Aaron arrive early at the synagogue for special selichot. On this day the rabbi does not blow the shofar. This is to show the difference between the month of Ellul and Rosh Hashanah itself.

The Greens prepare for Rosh Hashanah as for **Shabbat** (see page 36). They buy a fruit they have not eaten during the past season, such as a pomegranate. This is a symbol of renewal and the family will recite special blessings before they eat it. Just before sunset Mrs Green welcomes the holy day by lighting her candles (see page 40).

ROSH HASHANAH

The prayers for the evening service are addressed to God as a king sitting in judgement over His world. The prayers ask God to accept once more the monarchy of the world.

As the Greens leave the synagogue they exchange blessings with their friends. They say, 'May you be written down for a good year.' At home Mr Green says **kiddush**, then

they eat slices of apple dipped in honey to symbolize a sweet new year. They eat other symbolic foods, such as a fish head.

At the Rosh Hashanah morning service the shofar is sounded a hundred times. The rabbi blows three different notes. The three sounds represent different types of crying. The shofar is used to express the soul yearning to be reunited with God.

Later the Greens go to **tashlich** (casting away). This is a prayer asking God to remove the sins of His people. Jews say this prayer by the banks of a river or pond and throw bread on the water. This symbolizes the verse '...and You will cast all their sins into the depths of the sea...' (*Micah 7:19*).

THE TEN DAYS OF RETURNING

The ten days between Rosh Hashanah and Yom Kippur are called the ten days of returning. This is when Jews think seriously about how they have lived during the past year and resolve to do better in the year just beginning. Judaism teaches that God does not forgive a person until that person asks for forgiveness. Jews should also try to ask forgiveness from anyone they have wronged.

FACTFILE

The message of the shofar

The Jewish scholar Maimonides said that the message of the shofar was 'Awake you sleepers from your sleep, and you that are in slumber, rouse yourselves. Consider your ways, remember God, turn to him.'

In Israel, the swearing in of a new president is accompanied by blasts on the shofar.

A fish head – symbol of good deeds multiplying like fish

THE EVE OF YOM KIPPUR

The day before **Yom Kippur** there is an old custom of giving chickens to poor people for their pre-Yom Kippur meal. These represent the sacrifices in the ancient Temple. Today, many people give money instead.

In the afternoon Mr Green and Aaron go to the **mikveh**, the immersion pool. Usually only married women visit the mikveh (see Unit 40), but Yom Kippur is a special time when men are obliged to go. Immersion is for spiritual cleansing.

On Yom Kippur, Jews fast for 25 hours. Miriam is only eight so she does not have to fast. Pregnant women, women who have just had a baby, and people who a doctor thinks are not well enough to fast are also excused. Although Yom Kippur is a serious day, it is not a sad one. The Greens are happy to have the chance to make up for their sins (bad deeds). Their last meal before the fast begins is a festive occasion.

After the meal, the Greens get ready for evening prayers. They do not wear leather shoes, as these are a symbol of luxury. Mr Green wears a **kittel** over his clothes (see picture). This is to symbolize the verse 'Even if your sins are as red as scarlet they will become white as snow' (*Isaiah 1:18*). Mrs Green and the girls wear dresses that are mainly white. They do not wear any gold jewellery as this would remind them of the sin of the golden calf (see page 27). Just before sunset Mrs Green lights her candles.

YOM KIPPUR (DAY OF ATONEMENT)

This is the holiest day of the Jewish year and the synagogues are usually packed. Even Jews who do not go regularly feel the need to attend on this special day. Mr Green wears his **tallit** (see page 86). It is the only time the tallit is worn at an evening event.

Mr Green puts on his kittel

In the days of the Spanish inquisition, Jews had to accept Christianity or be killed. Many Jews made the vows, but secretly continued to observe the Jewish religion. Each year, just before Yom Kippur, they declared 'null and void' any vows they had made to the Christian Church. Today Jews chant the **Kol Nidrei** (annulment of vows) before the Yom Kippur prayers begin. It reminds them of the risks their ancestors took in order to keep their religion alive.

During prayers the members of the Green family confess their sins and ask God to forgive them. Jews only confess to God, never to a person. Jews think it shows disrespect to God to let other people hear about their sins. The prayer books help people to confess by printing lists of sins, like this:

'And so, may it be Your will, Lord our God and God of our fathers forgive and pardon us for all our transgressions (sins):

- for the sin which we have committed…under duress or willingly
- by hard-heartedness
- with an utterance of our lips
- with immorality
- openly or secretly
- with knowledge and deceit
- through speech…

People who know they have committed a particular sin must make a special confession of it. The Green family prays five times on Yom Kippur, starting with the evening service at the beginning of the fast.

The day of Yom Kippur begins with the morning service, followed by a reading of the Torah. This is *Leviticus 16* which tells about the Yom Kippur service in the ancient Temple. After this an extra service follows the Temple procedure step by step. Then there is a short break. At about midday Mrs Green takes Miriam home for lunch.

In the afternoon service the Torah reading from *Leviticus* warns the people of Israel not to be influenced by the ways of unbelievers. Then the book of *Jonah* is read.

The day's prayers end with **Neilah** 'the closing of the gates'. Throughout this service the doors of the Ark (see page 84) remain open. At the end of Neilah the Green family make three declarations of faith:

'Hear, O Israel, the Lord is our God, the Lord is One.'
They say this once.
'Blessed is the name of His glorious kingdom for ever and ever.'
They say this three times.
'The Lord is God.'
They say this seven times. The Israelites said this at the time of Elijah when they turned away from idols and devoted themselves entirely to God (*I Kings 18:39*).

At nightfall a single blast from the **shofar** tells everyone that the fast is over. They recite the evening prayer and then go home, where Mr Green makes **havdalah** (see page 39) and they all 'break' their fasts.

REFLECTION

'Fasting is something I do not enjoy. But Yom Kippur is different. I always feel so cleansed at the end of the day.'
(Mrs C, Manchester)

FACTFILE

At-one-ment

Atonement means bringing together those who have been separated – making them one (*at-one-ment*). On Yom Kippur, Jews express their awareness of the holiness, goodness and grace of God, compared with the sin and guilt of human beings.

In Biblical times, people would try to make up for their sins by making sacrifices to God. Animals to be sacrificed always had to be the best available. Sacrifice was not cheap. It was always meant to be costly.

Now that blood sacrifices no longer take place, Jews try to make *at-one-ment* by getting right with their neighbours, and getting right with God. Fasting is a personal sacrifice.

'Three times during the year all your males shall appear before the Lord your God,…on the feast of Unleavened Bread, the feast of Weeks and the feast of Tabernacles…'

(Deuteronomy 16:16)

THE PILGRIM FESTIVALS

The pilgrim festivals are **Pesach** or Passover (in spring), **Shavuot** or Weeks (summer) and **Sukkot** or Tabernacles (early autumn). In ancient times men used to go on pilgrimage to Jerusalem for these festivals. They usually took their families with them. Today Judaism does not have any pilgrimages so people celebrate the festivals at home or in the synagogue. Some like to visit Jerusalem at festival times so that they can pray by the Western Wall (see page 151).

The pilgrim festivals remember events in Israel's history:

- Pesach – the escape of the Israelites from slavery in Egypt
- Shavuot – when Moses received the **Torah** on Mount Sinai
- Sukkot – the journey of the Israelites through the desert on the way to the Promised Land.

For Jews living outside Israel the festivals last a day longer than in Israel. This began when Jews living in the **diaspora** could not know whether the new month had yet begun (see page 42) so they took an extra day for each festival. Today the extra day reminds Jews abroad that the Holy Land is very special.

HOW PESACH BEGAN

About 3500 years ago Jacob and his family settled in Egypt and soon grew into a large group. Egypt had been a rich and powerful nation, but now its empire was falling apart and there was widespread unemployment. A new king blamed all Egypt's troubles on the Israelites. He made them all his slaves. All the fit men had to work on building new cities or in the mines.

Then God chose Moses (who had fled from Egypt some years earlier) to go to Pharaoh, the king, and ask him to set the slaves free. Pharaoh refused, and God sent ten plagues to torment the Egyptians.

The last plague was terrible. God warned Moses that on a certain night the Angel of Death would kill all the firstborn sons of the Egyptians. The Israelites had to sacrifice sheep and goats and smear their blood on the doorposts of their houses. This showed the angel that they were Israelites and their children would be spared. That night death struck every Egyptian family. Pharaoh's firstborn son died. He begged Moses to go and to take the Israelites with him.

Then Pharaoh changed his mind. He went after the Israelites with a huge army. His 600 chariots raced over the desert in pursuit. The Israelites neared the shores of the Reed Sea (not the Red Sea). God sent a strong wind to drive the sea back. The Israelites passed over on dry ground. As the last of them reached the shore, the Egyptians chased after them. God reduced the wind and the sea came crashing back. Hundreds of Egyptians were drowned. The Israelites knew they were free.

PREPARING FOR PESACH

God ordered the Israelites to have an annual festival to mark this event. This festival was called Pesach. During it they were not to eat any **chametz** or have any in their houses. Chametz means leaven, that is, a substance in grain that makes bread or cake 'rise' when it is cooked. For Jews chametz is a symbol of pride, since it swells as it bakes. We talk of a person being 'puffed up' with pride.

Pride can lead a person to think they can do without God. At Pesach Jews remember that they rely totally on God, who took them out of slavery. They express this by having no chametz during the week of Pesach.

THE GOODMAN FAMILY PREPARE FOR PESACH

The Goodmans live in Glasgow. They spring-clean their house to remove all chametz. Michael (6) and Daniel (10) help their mother to clean out drawers and cupboards. Michael likes to use the nozzle of the vacuum cleaner to suck out dust from the sides of armchairs.

The kitchen receives special attention. This is because Pesach food must not be allowed to come into contact with appliances or utensils that have been used for preparing other food. Mrs Goodman cleans her oven with steel wool. She changes the cooker top and covers work surfaces. Mr Goodman cleans the sink. It is left unused for 24 hours, then he scalds it with boiling water and covers it with kitchen foil. Some Jews wash up in bowls.

Daniel searches for chametz with a candle and feather

The Goodmans bring out all the crockery, cutlery and saucepans that they use specially for Pesach. They lock away all the 'ordinary' things.

The Goodmans have stocked up with special Pesach food that is free from chametz. All the products must have the **hechsher** label '**Kosher** for Passover' (see page 70).

THE SEARCH FOR CHAMETZ

The **Bedikat chametz** (search for chametz) takes place on the evening of 14 **Nisan** (see page 35). Mrs Goodman hides ten pieces of chametz (usually bread) and Mr Goodman and the boys search for it, using a candle and feather (ancient versions of the torch and brush). They collect it in a paper bag. Next morning they have their last meal of chametz. Then Mr Goodman takes the paper bag into the garden, with its ten pieces of bread, and burns it on a bonfire.

FACTFILE

Moses

It is a miracle that Moses survived to lead the Israelites out of Egypt! When he was born the Pharaoh had ordered all Hebrew baby boys to be thrown into the River Nile. But Moses' mother hid him, then put him in a waterproof cradle among the reeds. His sister Miriam watched over him. An Egyptian princess found him and raised him as her son. When he was a young man he killed an Egyptian slave-master and had to run away. He lived in Midian for many years before God called him to lead the Israelites out of Egypt.

THE SEDER

As evening falls, Mrs Goodman lights her candles and welcomes the festival into her home (see page 37). Mr Goodman and the boys go to the synagogue to thank God for freeing their ancestors from slavery in Egypt. The table is laid with wine, three **matzot** (plural of **matzah**, unleavened bread), and a special plate like the one in the photo. Mr Goodman makes **kiddush** (see page 37) and the **seder** meal begins. Seder rhymes with 'raider' and means *order*. The meal has a set order in which Jews remember the slavery and departure from Egypt. This is written in the book they read at the seder, called the **hagadah** (telling). Michael, the youngest, asks four questions:

'Why is this night different from all other nights?

1 On all other nights we may eat chametz or matzah. Tonight why do we eat only matzah?
2 On all other nights we may eat any kind of herbs. Tonight why do we eat bitter herbs?
3 On all other nights we do not dip our food at all. Tonight why do we dip twice?
4 On all other nights we eat sitting or leaning. Tonight why do we all lean?

The Goodmans read the answers to these questions from the hagadah as the seder proceeds. Each item of food on the seder plate is a symbol to remind them of different parts of the story.

● *Matzah* This is the unleavened bread that the Israelites ate during their slavery. It bakes very quickly, so the Egyptians could

get more work from their slaves. When the Israelites left Egypt they had no time to bake proper bread. So matzah reminds them of both the food their ancestors ate as slaves, and the bread of freedom. It links together Jews who shared Pesach in the past, and those who will celebrate in the future.

- *Wine* During the seder everyone drinks four cups of wine. These stand for the four ways that God spoke about freeing the Israelites: 'I will bring you out', 'I will deliver you', 'I will redeem you', 'I will take you to Me' (*Exodus 6:6–7*). Red wine recalls the blood of the slaves who were beaten by the Egyptians. It also reminds Jews of the blood smeared on the doorposts of the houses when the firstborn sons of the Egyptians died.
- *Salt water* Some food is dipped in salt water that stands for the tears of the slaves. It also stands for the sea that drowned the Egyptians (see page 48).
- *Haroset* This is a kind of paste made from dried fruit and spices. It represents the mud bricks the Israelite slaves had to make.
- *Carpas* Jews usually use lettuce leaves or parsley for this. It stands for the way God provided fresh food for the Israelites in the wilderness. This is dipped in the salt water to remember the herbs that were dipped in blood and smeared on the doorposts.
- *Bitter herbs* This may be lettuce, a vegetable with a bitter root. It is a reminder of the bitterness of slavery.
- *Bone and egg* There is a burnt bone, either a neck bone of a chicken, or a shank-bone of lamb. This represents the sacrifices in the ancient Temple. The egg also stands for the Temple sacrifices, and is a symbol of new life.

The Goodmans also eat a proper dinner. They sing songs about how God helped the Jewish people. Before seder, Mr Goodman sets aside one of the pieces of matzah. At the end of the meal they eat this **afikomen** (dessert). It represents the food eaten after the Pesach sacrifice in the ancient Temple.

The Goodmans have another seder the next night. Jews in Israel only have one (see page 48).

THE REST OF PESACH

For the rest of Pesach the Goodman family eat only chametz-free foods. Mr Goodman does not go to work on the first two and last two days. The middle four days are 'ordinary days' when Jews may do some kinds of work.

On each day of Pesach the Goodmans go to the synagogue. They remember the Egyptians who died in the Reed Sea when the Israelites gained their freedom. They recall this by leaving out part of the joyous **Hallel** prayer (see page 42).

On the eighth day, after **havdalah** (see page 39), the Pesach utensils are packed away. The everyday things are put back. They can now eat chametz – and Mrs Goodman has a cake ready for them.

◇

RECIPE

Haroset
Ingredients:
4 tablespoons chopped mixed nuts
1 cooking apple, grated
1 teaspoon cinnamon
a little wine for mixing

Method:
Mix all the dry ingredients together and bind into a paste with the wine. Form into a flat round shape and place on the seder dish.

Shavuot celebrates the time when the Israelites received the **Torah** on Mount Sinai, seven weeks after their departure from Egypt. Jews think this is the most important event in human history. You can read about it in *Exodus 19–20*. The Bible describes how the Israelites were gathered round the foot of the mountain. Then thunder and lightning shook the sky. The voice of God called to Moses out of the thick cloud that surrounded the peak of the mountain. God gave Moses the Ten Commandments. Then Moses spent 40 days learning the rest of the Torah. When he returned, he was carrying the two blocks of stone with the Ten Commandments written on them.

COUNTING THE OMER

An **omer** is a measure of volume. It is about 2.25 litres. **Pesach** falls at the time of the barley harvest in the Holy Land. Jews count 49 days from the second day of Pesach until Shavuot, when the wheat harvest starts. This is called Counting the Omer. This is because during this period an omer of barley was offered in the Temple.

Shavuot did not have a fixed date in Biblical times. It depended on witnesses appearing before the Jewish court (see page 42) to say that a new month had begun. As months might have 29 or 30 days, Shavuot could have fallen on 5, 6 or 7 of **Sivan**. That is, on the fiftieth day after Pesach. Today, Shavuot always falls on 6 Sivan (and also 7 Sivan outside Israel, see page 48).

Shavuot starts in the evening, like all other festivals. However, while other festivals may begin before nightfall, on Shavuot the service begins after it is dark. This is because the Torah says that Jews must count seven *complete* weeks of the Omer. Complete means not only in days, but also in hours.

CELEBRATING SHAVUOT

There is no special **mitzvah** connected with Shavuot. This is because Jews feel that the gift of the Torah was of such overwhelming importance that no human action can represent or re-enact this event. The Torah is the link between God and the Israelites and the Jews of today.

In the Shavuot prayers Jews thank God for giving them the Torah. During the morning service they say **Hallel**. The Torah reading describes the scene at Mount Sinai when God gave the Torah to Moses and the Israelites. The Ten Commandments are read out (see page 26). In Israel, Shavuot lasts one day, but everywhere else it lasts for two (see page 48).

SOME SHAVUOT CUSTOMS

There are no special mitzvah, but some groups stay up all night at Shavuot to study the Torah. Some people recite tikun, a collection of readings from **Tenakh**, **Mishnah**, **Zohar** and other holy writings. They do this because Moses had to wake the Israelites to receive the **Torah**. Some Jews believe their ancestors were wrong to sleep. By staying up to study the Torah or recite tikun they are making amends for their ancestors' mistake.

The **Talmud** also says, 'A house in which the words of the Torah are heard at night will never be destroyed'. Jews believe that if they study through the night, they are preparing for the rebuilding of the Temple, which will never again be destroyed.

Synagogues are decorated with flowers for Shavuot, a joyful festival. Traditionally, dairy foods – especially cheesecake – are eaten. This is because the Israelites ate only dairy foods until they had learned the food laws concerned with the preparation of meat.

On Shavuot the synagogue is decorated with flowers

RECIPE

Cheesecake

For the topping:

225 g cream cheese
6 egg yolks
50 g melted butter
225 g caster sugar
vanilla essence
glace icing
20 cm square biscuit-crust pastry case

Method:

Tie the cream cheese in muslin and squeeze out the moisture. When the cheese is dry, crumble it into a mixing bowl. Add the egg yolks, melted butter, sugar and a little vanilla essence. Beat until the mixture is smooth. Place cheese mixture in case and bake at 180°C (gas mark 4) for about 1 hour. Leave to cool. Turn out, coat with glace icing. When set, cut into squares.

This recipe is a great favourite at Shavuot.

Sukkot takes place from 15 to 22 **Tishrei** (see page 35). The first two and last two days are holy. The middle four days are chol hamoed, 'ordinary days' of the festival. Jews can do some work during chol hamoed.

When the Israelites left Egypt they built temporary shelters in the desert. Some had tents. Some had to build small huts and covered them with leaves from palm trees. These were called sukkot. A sukkah was an ideal shelter in the desert. The leafy roof kept out heat and dust, but allowed air to circulate.

Today, Jews remember their ancestors' journey through the desert by building sukkot. They live in them for a whole week. The sukkah is a symbol of harmony, as it surrounds the family. Living in it strengthens a Jew's feeling of belonging to an ancient people.

◇

Debbie and David decorate their sukkah

BUILDING A SUKKAH – THE LEVY FAMILY

The Levy family of Manchester start to build their sukkah right after **Yom Kippur** (see page 47). Mr Levy builds it against the side of the house. Some families use their garden sheds which are fitted with lifting roofs.

A Sukkah must have at least three walls. These can be made from any material. It has to be high enough for a person to sit inside. The floor area can be as big as you like. A sukkah built in a synagogue yard could be large enough for a whole congregation.

The roof must be of any non-edible leaves taken from the ground or a tree. It must be thick enough not to let much sunlight through, but you must be able to see the sky. The sukkah must not be built under anything that cuts out the sky, such as a building or a tree. Mr Levy uses evergreens as other leaves dry out before the festival ends.

LIVING IN THE SUKKAH

The Levys live in their sukkah for the whole week of the festival. They eat their meals and invite visitors there. If it is warm enough, Mr and Mrs Levy sleep in the sukkah. They do this to remember their ancestors' journey (see page 34).

Debbie (aged 8) and David (aged 10) decorate the sukkah with paper chains and pictures they have drawn. They may buy coloured lights with their pocket money. Mr Levy likes to hang fruit from the leaves.

REFLECTION

'I like Sukkot. It's a bit like camping when we all go and eat outside. I like the leaves over my head and being with everyone else in the Sukkah.'

(Justin T, Northeast London)

THE FOUR SPECIES

Before Sukkot, Mr Levy buys his **arba'at haminim** (four species). These are: a citron (**etrog**), a palm branch (**lulav**), two sprigs of willow (**aravot**) and three branches of myrtle (**hadassim**). On each day of Sukkot except **Shabbat**, he holds them during part of the synagogue service. He holds the etrog in his left hand, and the others, bound together in a bunch, in his right.

Jews pray for rain at the end of Sukkot, as the four species are all plants that need water to thrive. While preparing for this, Mr Levy moves the plants to and from six directions towards his heart. This symbolizes God's presence and the blessings which He gives to all His creatures from every direction.

HOSHANAH RABBAH

Sukkot comes at the beginning of the rainy season in Israel. During the prayers for rain, they walk round the **bimah** in the synagogue (see page 84). They hold the four species. This is how it was in the ancient Temple (see page 7) when worshippers used to circle the altar. On the last day of chol hamoed, called **Hoshanah Rabbah**, they make seven circuits. This is the last time they say prayers for rain.

SIMCHAT TORAH (REJOICING OF THE TORAH)

The day following Sukkot is the day when **Torah** readings in the synagogue (see page 86) end and begin again. It is called **Simchat Torah**, or Rejoicing of the Torah.

This festival is also called **Shemini Atzeret** (Assembly of the Eighth Day). Outside the Holy Land where Sukkot lasts for eight days (see page 48), the eighth day is called Shemini Atzeret. The ninth is Simchat Torah.

Simchat Torah is one of the happiest days in the year. On this day all the synagogue's Torah scrolls are taken out. Some people dance round the synagogue with them while other people follow, singing and clapping their hands. Children wave flags. They go round the synagogue seven times. Children receive sweets and chocolates and a good time is had by all.

CHATAN TORAH AND BERESHIT

In Jewish tradition, the giving of the Torah on Mount Sinai is called the wedding of the Jewish people to God. God is the bridegroom and the Jewish people are His bride.

Before Simchat Torah two readers are chosen. The **Chatan Torah** (bridegroom of the Torah) will read the last portion from **Devarim** (*Deuteronomy*). Then the **Chatan Bereshit** (bridegroom of Genesis) will be called up to begin the new cycle of readings.

FACTFILE

The meaning of the four species

Many different meanings have been given to the four species or 'kinds'. The rabbis saw meanings connected with parts of the body, each of which can be used to serve God:

- *etrog* – heart – place of understanding and wisdom
- *palm* – spine – uprightness
- *myrtle* – eyes – enlightenment
- *willow* – mouth – prayer.

Body, mind and will combine to praise God, who is all around.

Hanukkah and Purim (see page 35) celebrate important events that the rabbis said should be remembered. They are called 'celebrations of the rabbis'.

HANUKKAH

The Prayer Book reminds Jews that this festival celebrates the miracle when God freed their ancestors from a powerful enemy.

Hanukkah (dedication) lasts for eight days and is celebrated in midwinter. It remembers the victory of a small Jewish army against the much greater forces of the Syrian Greeks in the second century BCE.

HOW HANUKKAH BEGAN

The Seleucid Empire

When Alexander the Great died in 323 BCE, his generals divided up the land he had conquered. One, named Seleucus, took the area from the Mediterranean Sea to the borders of India. This was the Seleucid Empire. The people in the region were of many different nations. Seleucus tried to get them all to Hellenize (adopt the Greek way of life) to make it easier to rule them. Quite soon, many began to dress like Greeks, speak Greek and worship the Greek gods.

Antiochus IV

Jewish society was divided. Some became Hellenists. They were opposed by Jews who refused to give up the ways of their ancestors. In 175 BCE, King Antiochus IV began to rule. He tried to force the Jews to Hellenize. He passed laws forbidding Jews from keeping the Sabbath or circumcising their sons (see page 72). He set up an idol in the Temple and ordered the Jews to sacrifice to it. Any who refused were tortured and killed. Despite this, many Jews showed great courage and kept firm in their religion.

The Maccabean Revolt

Antiochus sent soldiers to towns and villages in the countryside to force Jews to worship his idols. An elderly man, Mattathias, refused and killed a Greek officer. He and his sons fled to the hills. He became a national hero and other young men wanted to fight with him. He put his son, Judah, in charge. Soon they were fighting a guerrilla war against Antiochus' army. This became known as the Maccabean Revolt (see page 8). The name comes from Judah's nickname, Maccabi, which means 'hammer'. He was the 'Hammer of the Greeks'.

Restoring the Temple

After three years, Judah's forces drove out the Greeks. Their first priority was to restore the Temple. It was in a terrible condition. There was rubbish everywhere and weeds growing up between broken flagstones. While they were working, they found a small bottle of oil with its seal still intact. It was only enough for one day, but they filled the oil lamp. As they continued working, the lamp burned for eight days. Only when they had obtained fresh oil did the lamp go out. They knew this was a miracle. They realized the battles they had won were miracles, too. With God's help the few had overcome the many. The rabbis decided to hold an annual festival, when oil lamps would be lit and the Jews would sing praises to God.

HOW JEWS CELEBRATE HANUKKAH

For the eight days of Hanukkah, Jews attend the synagogue for special prayers, Torah readings and the reading of Hallel (see page 34). They light special lamps in memory of the event.

Jews remember that each day that passed made the miracle seem bigger. Oil that should only last one day burned for two, three and eventually for eight days. They express this by lighting a special oil lamp

Lighting an oil Hanukkah lamp

with holes for eight wicks in a row. This was the original Hanukkah lamp, or **hanukiah**. Today, many Jewish families use candles. The hanukiah has eight branches and a 'servant' candle. The Hanukkah lights are lit from this servant candle.

While the Hanukkah lamps burn, the women do no work. This is a way of honouring the Jewish women who showed such courage during the persecution of Antiochus. They circumcised their babies themselves when their men were too scared to disobey Antiochus. If they were caught, the baby was strangled and hung around its mother's neck. She was paraded through the streets as a warning to others. Despite this, the women continued to circumcise their sons.

Traditional foods eaten during Hanukkah are doughnuts and latkes, potato-cakes fried in oil. These help to remember the miracle of the oil.

During Hanukkah children play the game of **dreidle**. They use a spinning top with letters from the Hebrew alphabet on it. Children spin the top and make up words with the letter that falls uppermost when the dreidle stops spinning.

Children look forward to Hanukkah as this is when they receive presents and Hanukkah gelt – spending money.

THE IMPORTANCE OF HANUKKAH

Hanukkah is still important for Jews today. First it helps them to remember those who faced torture and death to keep God's commandments. Second, it shows God keeping His part of the Covenant (see page 22) and caring for His people.

KEY WORD

Hanukkah – dedication, a time when Jews remember that the Temple was cleansed and rededicated to God; they use this time to rededicate themselves to their religion

FACTFILE

Dreidle

On each of the four sides of the dreidle there is a Hebrew letter. The four letters are:

Nun – for Nes   *Hey* – for Hayyah
Gimmel – for Gadol *Shin* – for Shem

This spells out the sentence: Nes Gadol Hayyah Shem – 'A great miracle happened here.'

'And these days should be remembered and observed…so that the days of Purim should not pass away from among the Jews…'

(Esther 9:28)

Purim is celebrated in late winter. It is one of the happiest days of the Jewish year. It remembers how the Jews were saved from destruction about 2500 years ago. The story is in the Biblical book of *Esther*.

HOW PURIM BEGAN

Queen Esther

In 481 BCE Xerxes I (called Ahasuerus in the Bible) became King of Persia. Many Jews lived in the Persian Empire at that time. The book of Esther describes how Xerxes had his queen executed. Then he chose a Jewish girl, Esther, to replace her. Esther's uncle Mordecai used to visit her. He discovered a plot to assassinate the king. After the attempt to murder the king, a new prime minister was appointed. He was a foreigner named Haman, who was one of the 'Troublers of Judah and Benjamin'. These were enemies of the Jews. Haman wanted to use his new power to destroy the Jews. One day Mordecai refused to bow to him, and Haman used this excuse to report him to the king.

Haman casts lots

Haman accused the Jews of disobeying the laws of Persia, and the king allowed Haman to kill them all. Haman was very superstitious so he cast lots (like a lottery, *purim* in the Assyrian language). This was to choose the right day for the slaughter. He sent letters to the local governors throughout the empire ordering them not to interfere when the Jews' enemies killed them and stole their property. The Jews were not to be allowed to defend themselves.

The Jews are saved

Mordecai told Esther about the plot and she told Xerxes. He could not change the orders.

However, he loved Esther so much he had Haman executed and sent out new orders that the Jews could defend themselves.

The Jews fought bravely and by the end of the second day they had overcome their enemies and were safe. They celebrated with prayers of thanksgiving and feasts.

A year later Esther and Mordecai wrote to all the Jews in the Empire and told them to remember what had happened. The **rabbis** agreed, and the festival of Purim began.

HOW JEWS CELEBRATE PURIM

The Fast of Esther

Jews see Purim as a turning 'from anguish to joy, from mourning to festivity' (*Esther 9:22*). Their celebrations reflect this change.

The day before Purim is the Fast of Esther. Queen Esther ordered the Jews to fast for three days before she went to plead with the king. Jews fast in remembrance of this. It also remembers the days of fasting and praying when the Jews did not know what their future held.

During the fast there are special prayers and readings in the synagogue. Jews give to a special collection called **machazit hashekel** (the value of half a **shekel**). This is not directly connected with Purim, but with a tax which Jews used to pay toward the upkeep of the Temple. Now it goes towards the running costs of the synagogue.

Reading the Megillah

People come to the synagogue in their best **Shabbat** clothes on the evening as Purim begins. They are still fasting, but the joyous day has begun. They recite the evening prayers and read from the **Megillah** (scroll). This is a scroll of parchment which contains the book of Esther. Before the reading it is unrolled and folded so that it looks like a stack of pages. This is how royal orders were read in the Persian Empire.

During the reading of the Megillah, the congregation – especially children – stamp their feet and make a noise each time Haman's name is mentioned. This symbolizes blotting out the names of the Jews' enemies.

After hearing the Megillah everyone goes home to break their fasts and begin the evening parties. Next morning, after prayers, the Megilla is read a second time.

Gifts to the poor

Charity is important to Jews (see page 116). They believe it is especially important to make sure that the poor can also rejoice on happy occasions. Jews try to give in such a way that the giver does not know who receives the gift. The person who receives the gift does not know where it came from, either. At Purim children dress up and visit houses to collect for good causes. All gifts go to the charity organizers who give out the funds to those who are in need.

Sending food to friends

One of the best ways of making sure that everyone has enough food to celebrate is to send gifts of food to friends and neighbours. This way, rich and poor give and receive and all can accept without embarrassment.

Children taking Purim gifts to friends

The Purim meal

Purim prayers finish earlier than usual, so that people can go home and enjoy the celebration meal. Children wear fancy dress and there are usually guests to help the family to enjoy this happy occasion.

Shushan Purim

This is the day after Purim and remembers the struggle of the Jews of Shushan, capital of the Persian Empire, who did not overcome their enemies until the following day.

WHY PURIM IS IMPORTANT FOR JEWS

The **Talmud** says, 'If all the festivals should pass away, Purim would still be observed'. God is not mentioned at all in the book of Esther. The book seems to focus entirely on court affairs. But for Jews this teaches that God is there, behind the scenes, guiding events, even though His presence is not obvious.

FACTFILE

Making a noise

One of the instruments used for making a great deal of noise during the reading of the Megillah is called a *greggar*. This is a wooden rattle that has wooden slats in a frame. It is swung round a handle that has a ratchet. As each slat passes its cog on the ratchet, it makes a clacking noise.

It is similar to the football rattles that young men and boys used to take to matches to cheer on their side.

A scale model of the second Temple

'If I forget you, Jerusalem, may my right hand forget its skills.'

(Psalm 137:5)

Jews have had two Temples in Jerusalem. King Solomon built the first one 2900 years ago. The Babylonians destroyed it in 586 BCE. The second Temple, built on the same site, was destroyed by the Romans in 70 CE.

WHY THE TEMPLE IS IMPORTANT

(Read this section with Unit 39.)

For Jews the Temple was the holiest place in the world. It was always crowded. Pilgrims came from many countries at festival times. Of the 613 commandments (see page 22), 244 are about the Temple.

Jews regard the Temple as the place where God's presence could be felt. The **Mishnah** tells of miracles that happened there daily:

'…the rain did not put out the fire on the altar, the wind did not move the vertical column of smoke…when the people stood they were crowded together but when they bowed they had ample room…'

THE THREE WEEKS

On 17 **Tammuz** (see page 35) in 70 CE the Roman armies overran Jerusalem. After three weeks of fierce fighting the Jews were driven back to the Temple. On 9 **Av** the Temple was set on fire. These two days are fasts. The time between them is called 'the three weeks'. It is the saddest time of the Jewish year.

From 17 Tammuz Jews observe mourning customs (see page 81). They do not cut their hair or listen to music. No marriages take place. From the beginning of the month of Av they stop eating meat or drinking wine (except on Shabbat). This lasts until 9 Av and is called 'the nine days'.

TISHA B'AV (9 AV)

For Jews, 9 Av is a day of mourning. On this date both temples were destroyed. Many other tragedies in Jewish history also fell on this date. **Tisha b'Av** is a fast only second in importance to **Yom Kippur** (see page 46). From sunset on 8 Av until night falls on 9 Av, Jews do not eat or drink or wear leather shoes (see page 80). They do not have sexual relations. They only wash if they get dirty, not just to freshen up.

Late on 8 Av Jews eat seated on low chairs or on the ground (see page 80). They eat a hard-boiled egg, and dip bread in ash to remember the burning of the Temple.

The lights in the synagogue are low. The curtain is removed from in front of the Ark (see page 84). People do not greet one another. Prayers are recited quietly. The book of *Lamentations* (see page 28) is read in a sad chant. This describes the destruction of Jerusalem and the slaughter of its people.

Next morning, prayers are said quietly. Men put on their **tallit** and **tefillin** (see page 87) in the afternoon. After the service they read **kinot**, a collection of sad poems. These describe some of the suffering of Jews during their history. Some recall whole communities murdered in the Middle Ages. Others recall the **Holocaust** (1937–1945 CE, see page 16).

By midday people rise from their low mourners' seats and start working again. After nightfall they break their fasts. Some mourning customs continue the next day, as the Temple's ashes were still smouldering.

Although Tisha b'Av is sad, it is also a day of hope. Jews look forward to the Messianic Age (see page 24) when the Temple will be rebuilt.

THE FASTS OF TEVET AND GEDALIAH

The fasts of **Tevet** and **Gedaliah** remember the destruction of the first Temple.

Asarah b'Tevet, 10 Tevet, was the day when the Babylonians set siege to Jerusalem in 587 BCE. The Jews were starved into surrender.

The fast of Gedaliah happens on 3 **Tishrei**, the day after **Rosh Hashanah**. This is in memory of Gedaliah ben Achikam. He was a Jewish official who remained in Judea when thousands of others were deported to Babylon in 586 BCE. The Babylonians appointed Gedaliah over other Jews who remained. He was a man of peace and encouraged the Jews to take up farming and trade and to lay down their weapons.

On the second Rosh Hashanah after the destruction, a jealous Jewish prince killed Gedaliah. The remaining Jews fled to Egypt and all hope of rebuilding the Temple was lost.

KEEPING THE TEMPLE ALIVE

Jews keep the memory of the Temple alive in various ways.

- Prayers in the synagogues are read at the times when sacrifices in the Temple were offered (see page 86). The Temple is mentioned in all these prayers. **Torah**

readings on festivals describe the Temple sacrifices for those events.

- Bread is dipped in salt to recall the sacrifices that were sprinkled with salt before being placed on the altar.

- Psalm 137 is read before grace after meals on weekdays. This expresses the sadness of Jews exiled in Babylon.

- At the end of wedding ceremonies a glass is broken. This reminds Jews of the destruction of the temple.

FACTFILE

Psalm 137 – a pop 'hit'

Boney M, a pop group, recorded this psalm as a single in the early 1970s, and it was an instant hit. Here are some lines from this well-known psalm.

'By the waters of Babylon,
there we sat down and wept,
when we remembered **Zion**.
On the willows there
we hung up our lyres.
For there our captors
required of us songs,
and our tormentors, mirth, saying,
"Sing us one of the songs of Zion!"

But how can we sing the Lord's song
in a foreign land?'

THE NEW YEAR FOR TREES (15 SHEVAT)

The Bible tells farmers they must give a set portion of their crops as gifts for the priests and the poor. This is called tithing.

15 **Shevat** is the last date for all tithes of fruit. Fruit harvested after this date are tithed separately from crops from the previous year. This day is the New Year for Trees.

The **Talmud** says this is when the rainy season in Israel is over and the trees are beginning to produce their new crop of fruits. Jews believe that the cycle of the seasons shows that God cares for His world (see page 43).

The New Year for Trees is a happy event. Many Jews mark this day by eating different kinds of fruit. In Israel they plant trees.

LAG B'OMER (18 IYAR)

The 49 days after the second day of **Pesach** are called the Counting of the **Omer** (see page 52). The first 32 days are semi-mourning and many Jews do not cut their hair (see page 80) and no one may marry. The thirty-third day is called **Lag b'Omer** and is a happy day.

BACKGROUND TO LAG B'OMER

From the fall of Jerusalem in 70 CE to the **Bar Kokhba** revolt in 132 CE (see page 8) the Roman rulers of Israel were very harsh. During this time there was an epidemic (serious outbreak of disease) and in 32 days thousands of Jews died. Many of them were rabbinical students. It seemed that there would no leaders to guide the Jews through the difficult times ahead. On the thirty-third day of the Omer the plague stopped. Ever since, Jews have celebrated Lag b'Omer as a symbol of survival and hope.

On Lag b'Omer Jews cut their hair and marriages may again take place. Children are taken on picnics and outings. There may be parades with floats and bands (see photo on page 130). In Israel there are bonfires.

YOM HASHOAH (HOLOCAUST REMEMBRANCE DAY, 27 NISAN)

In 1933 the Nazi Party came to power in Germany and began persecuting the Jews. They published anti-Jewish propaganda, and passed laws depriving Jews of their rights.

Jews living in Germany and in countries occupied by German armies were rounded up and sent to concentration camps where they died. About six million Jews died in what is now called the Holocaust (see page 16).

Yom Hashoah – 27 **Nisan** – is Holocaust Remembrance Day when synagogues hold special services in memory of the Jews who perished. In Israel it is a very sad day and many Israelis give up their social activities. The armed services have special memorial services.

Yad Vashem is the Holocaust memorial in Jerusalem. The names of the concentration camps are engraved in Hebrew and English. Candles burn around them. There are photographs of the camps and the victims. Their clothing and other personal items, with photographs of camp life, executions and mass graves, are on display.

On Holocaust Remembrance Day many Jews visit Yad Vashem to light candles and recite psalms. Some **rabbis** preferred people to remember the Holocaust victims on **Tisha**

Sculpture at Yad Vashem

Independence Day celebrations in Israel

YOM YERUSHALAYIM (JERUSALEM DAY, 28 IYAR)

In 1948 after the War of Independence, the United Nations divided Jerusalem. Jews lived in the west and Arabs in the east (the Old City). The Western Wall (the only remaining part of the ancient Temple) was in the Arab sector. Jews could not visit it (see page 151).

On 28 Iyar 1967, after the Six Day War, the Israeli army entered the Old City. The **shofar** (see page 45) was blown at the Temple Wall and Jerusalem became one city. Jews and Arabs now have access to all parts of the city.

On 28 Iyar about 100 000 people gather at the Western Wall to pray and there are many celebrations and thanksgiving services.

b'Av (see page 60) when many sad events of Jewish history are called to mind. There are special prayers for the Holocaust victims.

YOM HA'ATZMAUT (ISRAEL INDEPENDENCE DAY, 5 IYAR)

After World War II, the survivors of the Holocaust urgently needed to have a home land. In November 1947 the United Nations divided Palestine into separate Arab and Jewish areas. The Arabs opposed the idea of a Jewish state.

British troops had been looking after the territory. As they left, the Jewish authorities declared the creation of the Jewish State of Israel (see page 13). The Arab states of Egypt, Iraq, Lebanon, Syria and Transjordan immediately attacked the new Jewish state. They wanted to destroy it. This became known as the War of Independence. It was a very fierce battle.

Since then, 5 **Iyar** has marked the celebration every year as **Yom Ha'atzmaut**, Israel Independence Day. It is a national holiday when schools, banks and businesses are closed and people go out on picnics. Jews are divided as to how it should be celebrated. Some synagogues hold services of thanksgiving and **Hallel** is recited (see page 42). In others no special service is held.

FACTFILE

Death camps

During World War II, hundreds of thousands of Jews were taken from their homes and deported to concentration camps in Poland. Millions died. There were concentration camps at Kulmhof, Belzec, Sobibor, Treblinka, Lublin and Auschwitz. Belzec used carbon monoxide gas chambers and 600 000 Jews died there. Sobibor accounted for 250 000, and Treblinka about 750 000. At Lublin about 50 000 were gassed or shot.

Auschwitz, near Krakow, was the largest camp. It used hydrogen cyanide gas to kill more than a million Jews. Gypsies and other prisoners also died. Victims came to Auschwitz from all over Nazi-occupied Europe. Hundreds of thousands of victims died from gassing, starvation, disease or shooting.

The family is very important to Jews. The home is where children learn about their faith. This is where parents show them what it means to be a Jew. They do this by their own example of daily living. Weekly Sabbaths and the cycle of festivals help children to identify with their Jewish roots. Children learn how even simple actions such as getting dressed or eating a meal can become holy, because these are ways of serving God.

THE DAY BEGINS

Sarah begins the day by saying 'thank you' to God for her waking up.

After this she pours water over her hands three times. She uses a jug and bowl placed beside her bed to do this. This is an act of purification, like the priests of Biblical times who washed their hands and feet before entering the Temple (see page 7). She thinks of each day as an opportunity to serve God, and therefore each day is a 'Temple'.

When she was very little, Sarah's parents washed her hands for her. Many Jewish parents do this every day. In this way children grow up in the habit of purifying themselves every day.

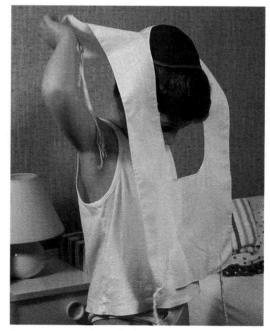

Simon puts on his tallit katan

GETTING DRESSED

In the photo above you can see Sarah's brother Simon putting on his **tallit katan** (small robe, see page 86). This is four-cornered garment, usually wool, with a hole for the head. It fits over the shoulders and drapes over the front and back of the body. On each corner are eight-fringed tassels called **tzizit** (fringes). Jewish men and boys wear it to follow the commandment '…They shall make for themselves fringes on the corners of their garments…and you shall see them and remember all the commandments of the Lord…' (*Numbers 15:38–39*). The tallit katan should be worn so that the fringes show, but some Jews tuck them inside their shirts.

Simon also wears a small cap, called a **kippah** (also called **kupple** or **yarmulke**). This shows respect for God. It reminds Simon that God's intelligence is greater than that of human beings. Married women may also cover their heads, as an act of modesty. Jews are forbidden to wear garments containing **shatnez**, a mixture of wool and linen (*Deuteronomy 22:11*). This is a **chukim** (see page 22) – a law for which no reason is given.

Sarah washes her hands

BLESSINGS

Jews pray three times each day. Men try to go to the synagogue to be part of the **minyan**. This is a group of ten men, and is the smallest number allowed for communal prayer. Simon usually goes with his father. Women do not have to go to the synagogue (see page 91), though some do. Sarah usually prays at home in the week. On Sabbaths and festivals everybody tries to go to the synagogue. There is more about prayer on pages 86–7.

As well as the set prayers, Sarah and Simon bless God before and after food. Each type of food has its special blessing. For example, before eating an apple they say, 'Blessed are You, Lord our God, King of the universe, who creates the fruit of the tree'. And before bread, 'Blessed are You, Lord our God, King of the universe, who brings bread out of the ground'. Bread has special importance, so Jews wash their hands before eating it (see page 37). They also say the full grace after eating bread. However, after all other food they only say a short 'thank you' blessing.

As well as blessings before and after food, Jews acknowledge God's power on many other occasions:

- on seeing lightning or hearing thunder
- on smelling fragrant flowers or herbs
- on seeing wonders of nature such as the sea, shooting stars and mountains.

Jews even bless God when they hear that someone has died. They say, 'Blessed are You, Lord our God, King of the universe, the true judge.'

In homes where children learn to say these blessings, it becomes natural for them to see opportunities for serving God in ordinary, everyday things.

PERSONAL STUDY

Jews are expected to learn about Jewish beliefs and practices. One of the 613 **mitzvot** is to set aside time to study the **Torah**. Most synagogues have study groups for both sexes, but some men prefer to study with a study-partner (**chavruta** system, see page 89). Parents help their children to study as soon as they begin to read Hebrew.

GOING TO BED

At the end of her day Sarah says the **Shema** (see page 18). She finishes '…may it be Your will…that You should lay me down in peace and raise me up to a good life and peace…'

FACTFILE

Hebrew

All observant Jews learn to read Hebrew as part of their religious studies.

Hebrew is one of the oldest written languages. The Hebrew alphabet has changed its appearance during the past 4000 years. It has 22 letters that represent consonants. In modern Hebrew vowels are shown by small marks above, under or alongside the consonants. Advanced readers do not need to use these marks. All Bibles are fully 'vowelled', but newspapers are not, so the readers must 'fill in' the vowel sounds for themselves.

Read more about Hebrew on pages 67, 75 and 152.

'And these words which I command you this day shall be upon your heart…and you shall write upon the doorposts of your houses and upon your gates.'

(Deuteronomy 6:9)

The photo below shows an object fixed to the right-hand doorpost. This is a **mezuzah** case, the sign of a Jewish house.

A mezuzah (plural **mezuzot**) is a scroll with passages from the Torah (*Deuteronomy 6:4–9* and *11:13–21*) written on it in Hebrew. They are the first two parts of the **Shema** (see page 18).

A mezuzah is handwritten by a trained **sofer** (scribe, see page 94) on parchment. Parchment is part of an animal skin, treated to make it smooth. Only the skin of a **kosher** animal (see page 68) can be used.

The parchment scroll hardly shows at all because it is in a protective case. Sometimes people wrongly think the case itself is the

Rolling a mezuzah to put it in its case

mezuzah. The mezuzah is the parchment scroll and the case is only to protect it from damp and dust.

WRITING A MEZUZAH

Before he writes a mezuzah, the sofer cuts the parchment into squares of different sizes, from 5 cm × 5 cm for a small Mezuzah to 15 cm × 15 cm for a large one. Then he scores lines lightly across to make sure the writing will be straight. He writes the letters below each line, as though they were hanging from them.

There are strict rules for the writing of a mezuzah. Every word must be written in the order they appear in the text. So, if a sofer writes a word wrongly and only discovers it later, he cannot simply go back and correct that word. This would result in his writing the corrected word after he had written the words that followed it. Instead he must erase everything from where he made the mistake and then write it all over again. If one of

The mezuzah case on the right-hand doorpost is a sign of a Jewish house

those words is the name of God, then it cannot be corrected. The name of God can never be erased. Mezuzot that cannot be corrected must be buried. They are buried with **tefillin** (see page 87) and damaged or worn-out sacred books in a Jewish cemetery.

When the mezuzah is complete, the sofer may give it to another sofer to check. Some soferim (plural of sofer) check their own. It is a great responsibility to ensure that people have perfect mezuzot.

Sadly, in recent years some dishonest people have been selling fake mezuzot. These are printed on parchment or paper treated to look like parchment. This is a mean thing to do, because Jews are tricked into buying worthless objects, thinking they are performing a **mitzvah**. A **rabbi** or trained sofer can spot such fakes easily – but it is not so easy for the untrained eye.

FIXING A MEZUZAH

The mezuzah is fixed to the doorposts of every room in a Jewish house and workplace except the bathroom and lavatory (these are not suitable places for a holy object).

The mezuzah is fixed on the right-hand doorpost as one enters the room. It should be in the upper third of the frame, but at least 10 cm from the top. It should slant a little inwardly towards the room. If the frame is too narrow, the mezuzah is placed vertically.

CARE OF THE MEZUZAH

Mezuzot are holy objects and must be looked after. Every three years Jews take down their mezuzot so that they can be checked by a rabbi or scribe. If the writing is faded, it can be written over with fresh ink. If it is damaged it must be replaced. It is a mistake not to take the mezuzah off the door frame before decorating. If paint gets in, the mezuzah will be ruined.

THE IMPORTANCE OF THE MEZUZAH

The mezuzah reminds everyone that everything that takes place within the house is done to serve God. It symbolizes the dedication of God and the Jewish people to one another. The mezuzah on each doorpost calls to mind the verse, 'You are blessed when you come in, you are blessed when you go out' (*Deuteronomy* 28:6).

FACTFILE

More about Hebrew

The names of the first letters of the Hebrew alphabet are *alef*, *bet*, *gimmel*. These sound like the Greek *alpha*, *beta*, *gamma*. The explanation is simple.

The ancient Israelites were great traders and travelled widely, especially during the reign of King Solomon (c. 971–931 BCE). They already had a written 'code' of sounds, rather than syllables, which most other peoples did not have. The Greeks were impressed by this invention and adapted it. Later, the Romans adapted it from the Greeks to form the Latin alphabet.

After the Jews were exiled from their land about 2000 years ago, Hebrew was limited mainly to prayer and Bible study. As a daily written and spoken language it remained 'dormant' until the beginning of the Zionist movement in the nineteenth century.

'…anything which has a completely split hoof and chews the cud, this you may eat…'

(Leviticus 11:2–3)

Kosher means 'fitting' or 'correct'. Food that Jewish people are permitted to eat is called kosher. This gives us the word kashrut, the state of being kosher. The opposite of kosher is **treifah**. All plants are kosher, but only some animals, birds and fish are. Animals must be killed in a special way and all the blood removed before Jews may eat the meat. Kosher does not mean food blessed by a **rabbi**.

KOSHER ANIMALS

Kosher animals must have hooves that are completely parted at the bottom to form two pads. They must also chew the cud. Cud is balls of grass that some animals form in their stomachs after grazing. Later they bring it back up into their mouths to chew it again before digesting it. Cows, sheep, goats and

Which of these are kosher?

deer have these two features and are kosher. Pigs, horses and camels are not kosher.

KOSHER POULTRY

There is no way of recognizing kosher birds. The **Torah** lists birds that are not kosher in *Leviticus 11:13–19*. This includes birds of prey. In practice, Jews only eat chicken, turkey and duck. Animals and birds of the right type can become **treifah** if they have anything wrong with them.

KILLING ANIMALS AND BIRDS (SHECHITAH)

(Read this section together with page 125.)

Jews may only eat animals and birds that have been killed by **shechitah**. Shechitah is a cut across the throat with a razor-sharp knife. Jewish law forbids causing pain to any

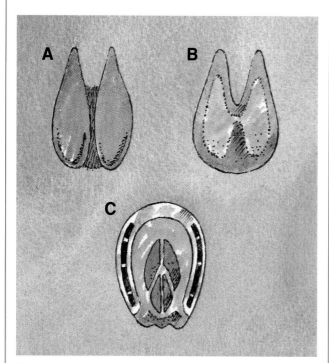

*Hoof prints of **A** cow, **B** camel and **C** horse – only **A** is completely parted*

creature. Shechitah is a painless and humane way of killing animals.

Shechitah is painless because the knife is so sharp and the stroke is so skillful. If you cut yourself on a blunt blade it would probably hurt quite a bit. But sometimes you can cut yourself and not even know it until the blood starts to flow. This is when the blade is very sharp. The shechitah knife is kept very, very sharp so that the animal does not feel the cut. The arteries that take blood to the brain are on either side of the neck. Cutting these causes the blood pressure in the brain to fall to zero. The animal immediately becomes unconscious and can no longer feel anything.

REMOVING THE BLOOD

The Torah says Jews must not eat the blood of animals and birds. If they find a blood spot in an egg, the egg is treifah and they throw it away. Jews use salt and water to remove blood from meat. This is how to do it.

1 Soak the meat in water for 30 minutes.

2 Lay the meat on wooden slats to allow the blood to drain away.

3 Sprinkle coarse salt over the whole of the meat. Leave for 1 hour to allow the blood to drip between the wooden slats.

4 Rinse the meat thoroughly several times to remove the salt. It is now ready for cooking.

This process is usually done by the butcher before the meat is sold. However, some people prefer to do their own salting so that their children can see how it is done.

Liver is different as it is difficult to remove the blood completely by salting. After sprinkling liver with salt they roast it over an open flame. This changes the nature of the blood.

FACTFILE

Non-kosher animals

Jews avoid eating non-kosher animals because God wills it. However, it can also be more healthy. For example, pig meat can harbour the eggs of tape-worms, and goes off very quickly if it is not refrigerated. This is important in hot climates.

KOSHER FISH

It is easy for Jews to recognize fish that are **kosher**. Fish that have fins and scales are kosher. All other seafood is forbidden. Jews may eat plaice, cod, herring, haddock, mackerel, salmon and tuna. Eels are not kosher as they have no scales. Shellfish such as crabs, lobsters and prawns are not permitted. Nor are octopus or squid.

LOOKING FOR INSECTS

For Jews, eating 'creepy crawlies' is not just horrible – it is a sin. Before they eat vegetables and fruit Jews must make sure they are completely free from insects.

Jews must wash leafy vegetables such as cabbage and lettuce carefully before eating them. Then they hold them up to the light and look closely under each fold. This enables them to ensure that all insects are removed.

The same applies to worms and maggots. These may get into fruit or vegetables. Children may help to search them out. Fruit damaged by maggots must not be eaten. Some kinds of fish may also have worms – these must be removed before cooking.

BUYING KOSHER FOOD

Jews can buy fruit, vegetables, eggs and most drinks anywhere. They buy fish from any fishmonger, provided the fish have fins and scales. They usually buy meat and poultry from a licensed kosher butcher. Some supermarkets sell kosher meat in sealed packs.

Some items such as soups, packet foods and sweets may contain ingredients that are not kosher. **Rabbis** sometimes supervise the manufacture of certain foods. They will certify the product is kosher by a printed label on the packet or carton. This label is called a **hechsher**. It reassures the Jew that the product is kosher.

Today many foods bear the hechsher. These include sweets, chocolates, biscuits, soup, margarine, oil, butter and cheese.

Kosher butchers' shops always display a licence from a board of rabbis. The board has to make sure that the butcher does everything properly. They send inspectors to check the shop. If the butcher is found selling non-kosher products, he will lose his licence immediately.

KOSHER RESTAURANTS

Kosher restaurants also have a licence from a board of rabbis. Kosher restaurants usually serve either meat or non-meat meals, e.g. fish or dairy food, but not both.

MEDICINES

Some medicines may contain non-kosher ingredients. These may be necessary to cure sick people and so the rules are relaxed. Many Jews prefer to consult a Jewish doctor or chemist. This is so they can be prescribed a kosher medicine, if it is available.

Some items of kosher food

Washing up – notice the bowl in the sink

IN A KOSHER KITCHEN

The Bible says, 'You must not cook a young goat in its mother's milk' (*Exodus 23:19*). Based on this, Jews who keep kosher homes do not eat meat and dairy foods at the same meal. A kosher kitchen has two parts: a meat section and a dairy section. Work surfaces are kept for either milk or meat foods. All crockery, cutlery and utensils are stored separately.

Jews keeping kosher homes find electric cookers easier than gas as spills will burn away. If they can afford it, they have two cookers or hobs, as well as two sinks. If they have only one sink, the family does their washing up in bowls. This is because a single sink cannot be kosher (everything gets poured down it). There is no need for two fridges or freezers as cold foods are not affected by the same rules.

Foods that are neither meat nor milk-based are **parev** or **parve** (rhymes with 'carver'). This includes vegetables, fruit and eggs. Parev foods can be eaten with either meat or milk.

RECIPE

A kosher recipe for quiche
Ingredients:
250 g ready-made shortcrust pastry
2–3 slices any kosher smoked sausage cut into small segments
150 ml soya milk
2 eggs, beaten
3 spring onions, chopped
salt and pepper
grated nutmeg

Method:
Roll out the pastry and line a 20 cm flan tin. Prick the base with a fork and bake blind at 200°C for 20 minutes. Leave until cool.

Arrange half the sausage segments in the case. Beat together soya milk, eggs and seasoning. Pour into the flan case. Lay the remaining segments on top to make a pattern. Arrange chopped spring onions in the centre. Grate nutmeg over the top. Bake at 190°C for about 25 minutes until the mixture is set. Serve with green salad.

RIGHTS OF PASSAGE

Rights of passage are ceremonies that mark the points when people pass (move) from one stage of life to the next.

CIRCUMCISION

> 'Then God said to Abraham, "...This is my covenant which you shall keep...you shall circumcise every male."'
>
> (Genesis 17:10)

Circumcision (**brit milah**) is the first Jewish rite of passage. It marks the entry of Jewish males into the covenant between God and the Jewish people (see page 22). It is also an important event in the life of a family. It links them through history to Abraham.

Circumcision means the removal of the foreskin. This is the skin that covers the tip of the penis. Circumcision is practised by many people, not only Jews. Many non-Jewish men are circumcised because the foreskin can become infected. Jewish circumcision is different from that carried out for medical reasons. This is because it is being done for a religious reason.

Jewish boys are usually circumcised when they are eight days old. It is done quickly and heals within a few days. If the baby is ill or too weak, the circumcision is put off until the baby is well enough. Jewish males who miss being circumcised in infancy must have it done when they are adult. Men who wish to convert to Judaism must be circumcised (see page 23).

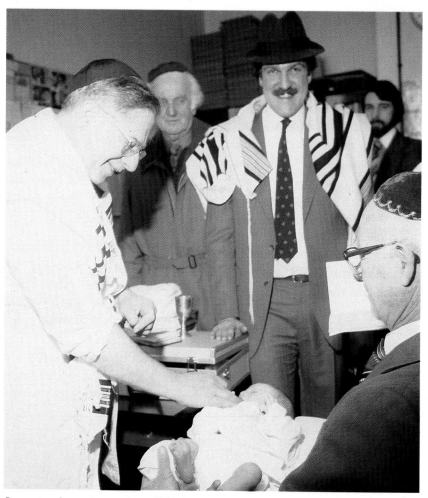

Preparing for a circumcision. Which man is the mohel and who is sandek?

Adult circumcision is more complicated than that of a child. It is carried out in hospital by a Jewish doctor who is qualified in Jewish (as opposed to medical) circumcision. It is carried out under local anaesthetic.

The person who performs infant circumcision is called a **mohel**. The mohel may be a doctor, but not necessarily. The mohel must be a very religious person. He has to know all the laws of circumcision and be trained in the procedure.

A circumcision is a happy event. Many babies are circumcised before they leave the maternity hospital (like the one in the photo). Circumcision may be performed at home or in the synagogue after morning prayers. Friends and relatives get together for a party.

THE CEREMONY

Before the ceremony the parents choose a man and a woman, usually a married couple, to act as **kvatters** or bearers. They carry the baby to his circumcision. The woman takes the baby from his mother and carries him on a cushion to the room where the men are waiting. She hands him over to her husband, who carries him to the mohel. There is an empty chair, the Chair of Elijah. An ancient tradition says that the spirit of Elijah visits every circumcision. The mohel places the child, still on his cushion, in the Chair of Elijah, for a moment.

Then the baby is placed on the lap of the man chosen as **sandek**. He is a respected member of the congregation, possibly the baby's grandfather. He holds the baby on his lap while the circumcision takes place.

As soon as the baby has been circumcised, the father thanks God that his son can enter the covenant through this operation. The mohel blesses the child and names him with the name the parents have chosen. The child is then returned to his mother by the kvatter and his wife.

After the ceremony there is a celebration meal.

NAMING GIRLS

Jewish girls receive their names in the synagogue on the Sabbath following their birth. Some **Sephardim** name their daughters at a ceremony called **zeved habat** (the gift of a daughter). This happens when she is seven days old. The **rabbi** blesses the baby and there is a celebration.

REDEMPTION OF THE FIRST BORN

Originally first-born sons were intended to be priests. Later only men of the tribe of Levi could be priests. Since first-born sons can no longer be priests, they must be 'redeemed', i.e. relieved of their priestly role.

When the boy is 30 days old, the father hands five silver coins (or an object of the same value), to a priest and 'buys' his son out of the priesthood. The child now has taken on a role he can fulfil – that of an ordinary Jew.

FACTFILE

Circumcision for health

In the USA and Britain, many males are circumcised for health reasons. About 90 per cent of American males are circumcised, though the number of babies being circumcised has dropped to about 60 per cent in the last decade. In Britain some 23 000 circumcisions are performed each year.

'Five is the age for starting to study scripture, ten for Mishnah, thirteen is the age for observing the commandments.'

(Ethics of the Fathers 5:21)

Bar mitzvah (son of the commandment) and **bat mitzvah** (daughter of the commandment) are names given to boys and girls when they become adults. It also means the ceremony that marks the second rite of passage – from childhood to adulthood.

JEWISH ADULTHOOD

For Jews 'adulthood' means people are able to be responsible for their actions. Jewish law says that age is twelve for a girl and thirteen for a boy. This is when a young person enters fully into the covenant relationship with God (see page 22).

BAR MITZVAH

Jewish families celebrate a boy's thirteenth birthday with a party. On the following **Shabbat** most boys will be called up to take part in the reading of the **Torah**. They may recite a blessing, or read part or the whole of the **sidra** (section, see page 38). Boys practise for weeks in preparation for this.

In some synagogues they must pass a test beforehand. Boys now start wearing **tefillin** (see page 87) and the **rabbi** will show them how to use them properly.

REFLECTION

'I was very nervous when I went up to read my part. My legs felt all wobbly. But it was all right once I got started. At the end I felt a bit sorry it was over.'

(David P. Brighton)

On the Shabbat when a boy is called up, friends and relatives come to the synagogue to hear him. Some may be called to recite a blessing on some part of the reading.

After he finishes his portion, the boy's father recites **baruch shepatarani**. He thanks God for raising the boy to maturity, and states that his son is now responsible for his own actions. The boy may then make a small speech accepting his responsibilities as an adult Jew. The rabbi may say some encouraging words to the boy in his sermon. There may be a small celebration in the hall of the synagogue afterwards.

Some bar mitzvah celebrations are very extensive, with banquets and balls. This goes against the Jewish teaching that this is a religious event, not an opportunity for costly showing-off. The celebration comes second in importance to the bar mitzvah itself. It is enough if family and friends meet for a meal, where rabbis and leaders of the community encourage the boy to continue to study and practise Judaism. The most important presents given are Jewish books (see page 89).

BAT MITZVAH

Bat mitzvah marks a girl becoming a woman. She becomes responsible for observing the commandments. As with the boys, any celebration comes second to the meaning of bat mitzvah itself.

It is only in recent years that Jewish families have begun to celebrate their daughters' bat mitzvah. Sharon had a party on her bat mitzvah and her friends were invited. She held this on a Shabbat afternoon in the summer. Her friend Naomi had hers in the winter when it got dark early (see page 34), so her party was after Shabbat.

In some **Sephardi** communities the father recites baruch shepatarani at this party. Sharon made a speech on a topic about

Sharon makes a speech at her bat chayil ceremony

Torah. Like her brother, she received gifts from friends and family. These included several Jewish books.

BAT CHAYIL

Most synagogues have a ceremony for girls who reach the age of twelve called **bat chayil** (daughter of excellence). Sharon studied the laws of Shabbat, festivals and **kashrut** (see page 68) as well as Jewish history, prayers and blessings. Her class visited a **mikveh** (see page 82). They took a test on all this before the ceremony.

Bat chayil usually happens on a Sunday. For Sharon the synagogue was decorated with flowers, and family and friends joined in the celebration. The **chazan** (prayer-leader, see page 93) sang accompanied by the choir. Sharon made a short speech and read a passage in Hebrew. The rabbi presented her with a **siddur** (prayer book, see page 86).

FACTFILE

The rebirth of Hebrew

Eliezer ben Yehuda (1858–1922) wanted to revive Hebrew as a living language. Using Hebrew roots he coined over 4000 new words to bring Hebrew into the modern era. In 1910 he began his *Complete Dictionary of Ancient and Modern Hebrew*. It was completed in 1959 after his death. Modern Hebrew (called Ivrit) was officially adopted as the language of Israel in 1948.

In American universities Hebrew was a compulsory subject. 'Commencement speakers' at Harvard and Yale were required to deliver their talks in Hebrew. Early grammar schools in England taught Hebrew and Greek. It is still taught today in many colleges and universities throughout the world.

'All the blessings that a man receives come to him only in the merit of his wife.'

(Talmud)

In Hebrew marriage is called **kiddushin** (sanctification, being made holy) or **nisuin** (elevation, being raised up).

Jews feel that unless people become part of a couple or a 'bonded pair' their personalities will not develop fully. The **Talmud** says, 'A man without a wife is incomplete'. Marriage is a very special relationship.

'The mating of animals is a...purely physical act. Through the sanctification of marriage however, a husband and wife become the closest of relatives.'

(Maimonides)

CHOOSING A PARTNER

A child born of a Jewish mother is Jewish. A child born to a non-Jewish mother is not a Jew even if the father is Jewish (but see page 141). Marriages between Jews and non-Jews may run into difficulties about how the children should be brought up. This is why it is important for Jews to marry a Jewish partner.

Jewish law forbids some marriages. Apart from the ban on marrying close blood relations, a **cohen** (priest, see page 25) may not marry a divorced woman, a convert or a woman whose father was not Jewish.

Many Jews choose their marriage partner by dating members of the opposite sex. In the more traditional Jewish communities people try to find out as much as they can about the background and character of the proposed partner before meeting them. If they seem suited, they meet. Then they can decide whether to develop a relationship. When partners are chosen like this, marriages are usually successful and divorces are rare.

PREPARING FOR THE WEDDING

A wedding can take place on any day except **Shabbat** or festivals. The bride tries to choose a day when she does not have her monthly period, as sexual relations are not allowed at that time. A few days before the wedding she visits the **mikveh**, an immersion pool (see page 82). Her mother or a close female friend goes with her. Sex before marriage is strictly forbidden.

On the Shabbat before the wedding the groom is called to the reading of the **Torah**. People throw nuts and sweets at him as a symbol of a sweet life.

THE WEDDING

Jewish weddings take place under a **huppah**, a canopy held up by four poles. This is a symbol of harmony. Sometimes weddings are held outdoors. The **rabbi** conducts the ceremony.

It is a happy day – but a solemn day, too. Both bride and groom fast until after the ceremony. In their afternoon prayers, they confess their sins and ask forgiveness.

An outdoor wedding: bride and groom leaving the huppah

The marriage ceremony

1 Birchat eirusin (initial blessings)
The rabbi recites two blessings over a cup of wine. The first is the usual blessing over wine. The second praises God for giving the people of Israel marriage. The bride and groom then drink from the same cup.

2 The ring
The groom places a ring on the bride's finger and says (in Hebrew), 'With this ring you are sanctified to me according to the Law of Moses and Israel'.

3 Reading of the ketubah
The **ketubah** (marriage contract) says that the husband intends to feed, clothe and care for his wife. It is usually written in Aramaic, a language similar to Hebrew (see page 152). A brief English version may be read. In **Sephardi** weddings the ketubah is read to the groom before the ceremony begins.

4 Birchat nisuin (the final blessings)
The rabbi recites seven blessings, praising God for creating the human race, giving joy and gladness and bringing happiness to the couple. After the ceremony the groom breaks a glass, wrapped in a cloth, with his foot. This reminds them of the destruction of the Temple (see page 61).

5 Yichud (private togetherness)
Straight after the ceremony the bride and groom go to a private room. They can be alone together for a short while. They break their fast and have a few relaxing moments.

6 Shiva b'rachot (seven blessings)
Traditionally the wedding celebrations go on for a whole week with a feast every night in the homes of different people. At the end of each meal the seven blessings are recited.

TAHARAT HAMISHPACHA (FAMILY PURITY)

(Read pages 82–3 with this section.)

The couple must observe the Jewish law of family purity. Judaism strictly forbids sexual relations during menstruation. Each month, from the time her period starts until she has immersed in a mikveh (see page 83) a wife is in a state of **nidah**. This means she is separate from her husband. She is nidah through the whole of her period and seven days afterwards. It is always twelve days or more. During this time there can be no physical contact between the couple. When she returns from the mikveh, they can resume the sexual side of marriage.

The value of this separation is that it is like being engaged again. They can express their love in non-physical ways. It helps to make a marriage strong. Each time the wife comes back from the mikveh, it is like starting their marriage anew. The Talmud describes it as being under the huppah all over again.

FACTFILE

Some marriage symbols
The huppah is said to represent the new home the couple will share together. In ancient times huppah was the name of the bridal chamber where the marriage could be consummated.

The ring may date back to the times when a husband gave his wife precious jewels as a marriage gift. As in other religions, its shape, a circle – a line that never ends – represents eternal faithfulness. It is made from metals that do not tarnish. This means their love will remain pure.

'Whoever divorces his first wife, even the altar sheds tears on her behalf.'

(Talmud)

Jews value marriage very much. If a marriage seems to be in trouble, they will do all they can to save it. However, Judaism realizes that in some cases divorce is the only proper solution. A Jewish document of divorce is called a **get**.

GROUNDS FOR DIVORCE

A Jewish couple do not have to prove grounds for divorce. If the couple have tried to save their marriage and finally agree to a divorce, they can do it with no real problems. If more Jewish people knew how simple their divorce process is, they would probably have a Jewish divorce as well as a civil one. There are no objections to divorced people remarrying.

Only the **cohen** (priest, see page 25) is not allowed to marry a divorced woman.

THE GET (DOCUMENT OF DIVORCE)

The get certifies that a marriage has been terminated. A scribe (see page 94) must write it on parchment. A get is a very precise document. It has to include every name that the husband and wife might be known by. It must say clearly where and when the divorce took place. The get is the property of the woman, but usually the **bet din** (Jewish court, see page 97) keeps it. The bet din will give the wife a certificate that she needs to produce if she wishes to remarry at any time.

DIVORCE PROCEDURE

When a couple have agreed to divorce, the husband applies to a bet din for a get. They attend at a date fixed for them. The scribe writes the get in front of the **dayanim** (judges) and the husband hands it to the wife in front of two witnesses. If the couple do not wish to face each other, either of them can appoint a representative to give or receive the get. The divorce is valid as soon as the wife or her representative receives the get.

If the couple live in different towns or countries, the husband applies for the get at his nearest bet din. It is then delivered to the bet din in the town where the wife lives. She is asked to attend the bet din to receive the get in front of witnesses.

In most countries the get is issued after the civil divorce. In Israel the Jewish divorce is the civil divorce.

A couple who divorce in a civil court are still married in Jewish law. If they marry new partners without a get they are committing adultery.

Reading the get in the bet din (c. 1920)

MAMZERIM

If a woman remarries without having a get, the second husband will be living with a woman who is still married to someone else.

A child born from a relationship like this is a **mamzer** (plural mamzerim). Judaism does not regard a child born to unmarried parents as a mamzer. A mamzer is born to a married woman who has committed adultery. This is very sad, as mamzerim can never marry a Jewish partner, and this is through no fault of their own.

THE AGUNAH

It is also very sad if a husband is missing, but the wife has no proof that he is dead. The woman is known as **agunah**, a 'chained wife'. She cannot remarry until such proof can be produced.

Rabbis go to great lengths to free agunot (plural of agunah) from their situation. They will accept any reliable evidence that the husband is dead. After the **Holocaust** (see page 16) rabbis were very easygoing in freeing agunot from missing husbands.

If a man refused to give his wife a get, she also becomes agunah and cannot remarry. If she does she becomes an adulteress. A bet din cannot force a man to give a get. A husband must give it of his own free will. Similarly, a wife may refuse to accept a get and the bet din can do nothing. A get is only valid if it is freely given and freely accepted.

Today, some rabbis try to write a prenuptial agreement into the marriage document. This is where both bride and groom agree that if the marriage breaks down they will not refuse to give or to receive a get. This is not easy. If the case went to a court of law, it would mean the get was not freely given or accepted.

FACTFILE

Civil divorce

Except in Israel, Jews must obtain a civil divorce as well as the get.

In Britain a couple must usually have been married for a year before they can apply for a divorce. They must show that the marriage has 'irretrievably broken down', that is, the marriage is dead.

Evidence of the breakdown is:
- unfaithfulness (adultery)
- cruelty, mental or physical
- unreasonable behaviour
- desertion (a partner is absent for 2 years).

POINTS OF VIEW

Many Jews feel that it is unfair that women have to rely on their husbands giving them a get or that husbands have to rely on their wives accepting one.

'When a man leaves this world, [no riches] accompany him, but only the **Torah** he has learnt and the good works he has carried out.'

(Ethics of the Fathers)

We all feel grief when someone we love dies. The Jewish mourning customs help people to grieve and gradually return to normal life.

THE DYING PERSON

Jewish families come together to be near a loved one who is dying. If possible a person should spend their last moments confessing their sins and reciting the **Shema** (see page 18). Jews think it is a great kindness to stay with a person at the moment of death and make sure the eyes are closed. Those present then bless God as 'the true judge' (see page 65) and tear a small piece of their clothes as a sign of grief (*Genesis 37:34*).

A MOURNER BEFORE THE BURIAL (ONAN)

From the time of death until the body is buried a mourner is known as an **onan** (immediate mourner). The onan's first priority is to arrange the burial. Jewish law forbids cremation (but see page 138). It is disrespectful to delay a burial or to leave a dead person alone. Someone stays with the body until the funeral, even if it is in a mortuary.

THE FUNERAL

As soon as a doctor has signed a death certificate the **chevra kaddisha** (burial society) prepare the body for burial. They wash the body and immerse it in a **mikveh** (see page 82). This is not the same mikveh used by living people. Men wash male bodies, women wash female bodies. They wrap the body in a plain linen shroud (burial cloth). A man is usually buried wearing his **tallit** (see page 86). The body is then placed

in a plain, unpolished wooden box. There are no brass handles or internal padding. In death, rich and poor are treated alike.

The funeral is simple. Some psalms are read, then there is a short prayer praising God for granting life and taking it away. A **rabbi** may give a short speech about the dead person. There is no idle chatter as this is thought to be disrespectful. **Sephardim** walk seven times round the coffin and recite prayers for angels of mercy to accompany the soul. The coffin is then lowered into the grave and earth is piled on top of it. People offer words of comfort to the mourners and then all go and wash their hands before leaving the cemetery.

From now on the mourner is not an onan, but an **avel** (plural avelim), a prolonged mourner. At home the avelim eat a meal of hard-boiled eggs. The egg has no opening and this symbolizes the mourner's inability to open their mouths to put their grief into words.

THE FIRST WEEK (SHIVA)

The first week after the funeral is called **shiva** (meaning seven). It is the most intense period of mourning. The avelim stay in one of their homes and do not leave it unless absolutely necessary. Friends and members of the synagogue visit to pray with the mourners three times a day (see page 86). The male members recite **kaddish**. In this they declare

God's greatness and pray for the coming age of universal peace (see page 24).

During shiva the mourners sit on low chairs (see page 60) except on **Shabbat** when no mourning is allowed. They do not cut their hair or nails. All mirrors are covered so that people do not think about their appearance, and no sex is allowed. They do not listen to music, and do not wear leather shoes. A candle is kept burning night and day to remember the verse, 'A person's soul is the candle of the Lord' (*Proverbs 20:27*). At the end of the week the family return to their normal daily routines.

THE FIRST MONTH (SHELOSHIM)

Sheloshim (thirty) is the first month of mourning and includes the week of shiva.

A mourner during shiva. How many mourning customs can you see in the picture?

After shiva the worst part of mourning is over and things begin to return to normal. The male mourners go to the synagogue each day to recite kaddish.

Some families try to have a headstone set in place by the end of sheloshim. Others leave it until a year has passed. Sephardim usually have a flat stone slab covering the whole grave instead of a headstone.

Jews mourning their parents are avelim for the first year. They do not play or listen to music, except for professional musicians who depend on it for their living. Kaddish is said for eleven months. On the anniversary of the death, called **yarzheit** (a Yiddish word), a candle is lit and burns through the night and day and the men say kaddish. The relatives repeat this every yarzheit.

FACTFILE

Some symbols of mourning

Jewish belief about life after death is shown in their name for a cemetery – *Bet Hahayyim*, the House of Life.

Keriah, the tearing of the garment, refers to the time when Jacob tore his clothes when he was told that his son Joseph had died (*Genesis 37:34*).

Sitting on low stools symbolizes that the whole body is 'brought low' by grief.

Not looking in mirrors, not cutting hair and nails all represent deep sadness, and the feeling that the mourners must focus their whole minds on mourning their lost one.

'The principles of purity and impurity...are among the Chukim.'

(Maimonides)

(Chukim – laws for which no reason is given.)

Mikveh (plural mikvaot) means 'a place where water has gathered'. For Jews this is a special pool where people can immerse, or dip themselves, to be purified. The laws of family purity (see page 77) need a mikveh. These laws are so important that a Jewish community must build a mikveh before they build a synagogue.

THE IMPORTANCE OF THE MIKVEH

In ancient times people visited the Temple to bring sacrifices and other gifts (see page 7). This meant they always had to be pure.

Inside a mikveh. Steps lead down to the immersion pool

Touching a corpse or a dead animal (except those killed for food or sacrifice) made a person impure. Menstruation (monthly periods) also made women impure. People could become pure again only by immersing themselves in natural water.

People could use rivers or ponds, but generally visited the mikveh – a special pool where rainwater had collected.

Now that there is no Temple, the mikveh is mainly visited by Jewish women after menstruation and childbirth.

Men must visit the mikveh the day before **Yom Kippur** (see page 46). Some also go on the evening of **Shabbat** and festivals. Non-Jews converting to Judaism must also immerse in a mikveh (see page 23).

PURITY AND IMPURITY

Taharah and **tumah** are often translated as 'purity' and 'impurity'. It is sometimes difficult to translate words from one language to another so that they mean the same. 'Purity' and 'impurity' are not about personal hygiene but refer to spiritual purity. You should bear this in mind when you read this unit.

THE STRUCTURE OF A MIKVEH

A mikveh is a tiled pool and may be 3 to 5 metres long and from 2 to 3 metres wide. It contains 350 litres or more of water. There are stairs with a hand rail leading down into the water.

In ancient times the mikveh was filled with rain water. Today the immersion pool is filled with tap water. A pipe connects it to a pool filled with rainwater. The pool is drained and cleaned each day, and the water is heated.

MIKVEH FOR MEN

Men have a separate mikveh from the women. There are changing rooms and showers. They must be physically clean before going down into the mikveh.

THE WOMEN'S MIKVEH

This is much more pleasant than the men's. There are private bathrooms with showers leading into the mikveh area.

A week after her period has ended, a woman is ready for the mikveh. This usually takes place after dark. When she arrives at the mikveh, she waits for a bathroom so that she can begin her preparation.

The woman must remove nail polish, rings and other jewellery. Nothing must come between her body and the water. When the woman is ready, a female attendant calls her to go down, in turn.

Then she goes into the pool and immerses. The female attendant watches to ensure she has done it properly (see page 9). She folds her arms and, while the attendant puts a towel over her hair, recites a blessing. She then immerses a second time. When this is done she returns to her 'pure' state and is ready to resume sexual relations with her husband.

TRENDS IN MIKVEH ATTENDANCE

History shows that many women have gone to great lengths to maintain the tradition of the mikveh. However, in the early twentieth century, mikveh attendance began to decline.

This was because many Jews who came to the west as refugees before World War I began to drop their Jewish practices. Young women began to think the mikveh was a means of keeping clean. They felt they could wash in their own bathrooms. Today, mikveh attendance is increasing as more women are discovering the importance of the monthly immersion.

IMMERSING UTENSILS

Not only people are dipped in the mikveh. New kitchen utensils and tableware must also be immersed, unless they were manufactured by a Jewish firm. All labels and makers' marks must first be removed.

Mikvaot for utensils are different from the ones people use. They can contain only rain water, as the utensils can be washed again afterwards. It is also safer to immerse tableware in a separate mikveh. A broken glass or cup on the mikveh floor would be a hazard to anyone coming to immerse.

FACTFILE

The mikveh in history

About 48 km (30 miles) from Jerusalem stand the ancient ruins of Masada on top of a steep mountain. When the Romans drove the Jews from Jerusalem in 70 CE about 1000 Jewish men, women and children fled to the fortified palaces on this sheer mountain top. With their leader, Eleazer ben Jair, they withstood a two-year siege by the Roman Tenth Legion. When the Romans captured Masada, the Jews killed themselves rather than surrender.

When archaeologist Yigael Yadin excavated the site in 1963–65 he discovered the mikveh the women used, even while under siege.

God asks, 'Did anyone ever enter a synagogue and not find My presence there?'

(Midrash)

A synagogue is a Jewish house of worship. **Ashkenazim** call it schul (rhymes with 'pool'). **Sephardim** usually call it **Bet ha Knesset** (house of assembly).

HOW SYNAGOGUES BEGAN

Most historians think that when Jews were deported to Babylon about 2500 years ago, they began to meet in each other's houses to pray and to study the **Torah**. Later they set aside special buildings for prayer, and these were the first synagogues.

THE LAYOUT OF THE TEMPLE

The first 'house of worship' of the Jews was the portable Sanctuary made of posts, boards and curtains that they carried around with them in the desert (see page 7). The Israelites set it up whenever they encamped. You can read about this in *Exodus 25–30*. There was a large rectangular enclosure. Inside this was a washstand where priests could wash before starting a service and an altar where they sacrificed animals. Beyond that was a tent called the Holy Place. Only priests were allowed in it. Deep inside the Holy Place was a parochet (a screen) that hid another room called the Holy of Holies. The Holy of Holies contained the Ark, a wooden box covered with gold. The Ark held the stone blocks with the Ten Commandments carved on them (see page 26).

King Solomon's Temple was based on the layout of the Sanctuary, but made of stone. Instead of cloth screens there were walls and a courtyard. The Holy Place and Holy of Holies were also made of stone. King Solomen added another courtyard where women could pray.

Inside a modern synagogue

SYNAGOGUES TODAY

Synagogues are based on the design of Solomon's Temple. They face towards Jerusalem where the Temple stood. At the entrance there is a sink for worshippers to wash their hands before prayer. There are separate seating areas for men and women (but see page 138).

At the front of the synagogue there is a large cupboard or recess covered by the parochet (screen). This is the **Aron hakodesh** (the Holy Ark) and represents the golden box in the Temple. Inside it are the scrolls of the Torah, the holiest objects in the synagogue.

In the centre of the synagogue is a raised platform called a **bimah**. The reader places the Torah scroll on a table and reads the **sidra** from here. This is like the platform in the Temple from which the Torah was read.

Above the Ark the **ner tamid**, the 'perpetual light' burns. This represents the **menorah**, the oil lamp of the Temple, and is never put out. The menorah had seven wicks and one of them is kept burning continually. Near the ner tamid may be a stone or bronze plaque with the Ten Commandments carved on it.

On one side of the Ark is the **rabbi's** seat, and on the other a seat for the **chazan** or a visiting speaker. There is usually a pulpit, where speakers stand to give their sermons.

These features are all standard in most synagogues, but the design and decoration of synagogues vary greatly. Jewish law forbids images in sculpture or pictures, so none are found in a synagogue. Some synagogues may have two lions embroidered on the parochet. The lion represents the tribe of Judah from which the Messiah is expected to come (see page 24).

SEFER TORAH – THE TORAH SCROLL

Torah scrolls are made from animal skins stitched together to form a long strip for writing on. The Five Books of Moses (see page 26) are written on these skins in columns. There are 250 columns to each Torah scroll, which is about 60 metres long. Each end is stitched to a wooden roller called an **etz chaim** (tree of life). The etz chaim are used for winding the scrolls to the part to be read. Writing a scroll takes about 1000 working hours, and is the task of a trained scribe (see page 94).

The scrolls are kept in the Ark. In Ashkenazi synagogues the scrolls are tightly bound with silk or velvet binders and dressed with velvet mantles. The Sephardim keep them in wooden cases (see page 27) covered with silk, and decorated with silver ornaments.

USES OF THE SYNAGOGUE

In ancient times synagogues were used as classrooms and the local **bet din** (rabbinic court, see page 97) might have met in an adjoining building. There were often guest rooms for visitors, and **mikveh** (see page 82).

Modern synagogues usually have classrooms, and a community hall for holding weddings and **bar mitzvah** celebrations, as well as for meetings and lectures. Other rooms are used for mother and toddler groups, senior citizens' clubs and so on. Bet din no longer

meet at synagogues, and most synagogues do not have a mikveh attached.

Youth activities, such as youth clubs, scouts and guide groups, and holiday activity groups, also meet on synagogue premises. Regular adult study groups also take place there, as well as lectures by visiting speakers.

KEY WORD

Synagogue – from a Greek word meaning to come together

FACTFILE

A new Torah scroll

The presentation of a new Torah scroll is a great occasion. The scroll has taken perhaps a year to write by a trained **sofer** (scribe). It costs several thousand pounds.

On the day of its presentation, the writing of the last words is completed. Individuals are honoured by being allowed to write one of the last letters.

The new scroll is carried through the street under a **huppah** (bridal canopy) accompanied by people carrying candles and singing. All the other scrolls are also taken from the Ark into the street. All the scrolls are then carried in a singing, dancing procession that continues round the synagogue, as on **Simchat Torah** (see page 55).

Jews believe that a person can pray to God at any time and in any place. In the **Tenakh** and the **Talmud** there are examples of people simply speaking their thoughts and feelings to God. There are also set prayers based on the ancient worship in the Temple.

Jews consider both types of prayer are important. People can pray informally with great devotion. But if people only spoke to God when they needed to, they would not pray very often. Set prayers provide a framework of regular times for turning to God.

A Jewish prayer book is called a **siddur**. It contains the set prayers. A siddur is printed in Hebrew, as Jews think of Hebrew as **leshon hakodesh** 'the holy language', the most suitable language for prayer. Each book usually has a page-by-page translation so that people can also pray in a language they understand.

DAILY PRAYERS

Each day in the synagogue there are three services:

- **shacharit** – morning prayer
- **minchah** – afternoon prayer
- **arvit** – evening prayer.

Jewish tradition links these times with the Patriarchs.

- Abraham started his day with prayer.
- Isaac prayed in the afternoon.
- Jacob prayed in the evening to thank God for helping him through the day.

Prayer in the synagogue coincides with the times when Jews used to offer sacrifices in the Temple.

On new moons and festivals an extra service (**musaf**) is said at the time when Jews used to offer an additional sacrifice for these events.

REFLECTION

'I travel a lot, and can't always get to **shul** [synagogue] in the mornings. Those mornings when I do go, I feel really alive.'

(Mr F, Sale)

The most important Jewish prayer is the **Shema** (rhymes with 'bazaar'). It contains three parts: *Deuteronomy 6:4–9* and *11:13–21* and *Numbers 15:37–41*. It begins with a statement that God is one, then Jews pledge themselves to accept God's rule and keep His commandments. Jews recite the Shema in morning and evening services, and again before going to sleep (see page 65).

The **Torah** is read on **Shabbat** and festivals, and on Monday and Thursday mornings. This began for the farmers who came into town on these days for the markets. Continuing this habit ensures that people do not go more than three days without hearing the Torah.

For parts of the service and the Torah readings there must be ten Jewish males over the age of thirteen present. This is a **minyan** (required number). Prayers can be said without a minyan, but some parts are omitted.

THE TALLIT (PRAYER ROBE)

During morning prayers Jewish males wear a **tallit** and **tefillin** (see opposite). The full name is **tallit gadol** (large robe), to distinguish it from the **tallit katan** (small robe, see page 64).

The tallit is a square or rectangle of white cloth, usually made of wool or silk. Attached to each corner are fringes called **tzizit**. These are the same as the fringes on the tallit katan. Recently some men have begun wearing a very small tallit like a scarf. This has led to the tallit being called a 'prayer shawl' which is incorrect. A tallit should be

Boy wearing tallit and tefillin

are small parchment scrolls containing four sections from the Bible. These are the first two paragraphs of the Shema and *Exodus 13:1–10* and *13:11–16*. The scrolls are handwritten by a trained scribe (see page 94). The boxes are sewn up with sinews. Every part of the tefillin – parchment scrolls, boxes, stitching and straps – must be from the skin of **kosher** animals (see page 68).

The wearing of tefillin is symbolic. The arm tefillah is bound round the top of the biceps muscle of the left arm (or right arm for a left-handed person). With the arm at rest, the tefillah lies next to the heart. This reminds the wearer that he serves God with his heart. The head tefillah reminds him he must serve God with his mind.

Tefillin are holy objects for Jews. They have to be checked every three years to make sure the writing has not faded or cracked. This is done by a qualified scribe (see page 94).

big enough to cover a man's whole body, as it is also used as the shroud in which he will eventually be buried (see page 97). A full-size tallit is about 2 metres by 1.5 metres. Customs vary from synagogue to synagogue as to the wearing of tallitot.

A tallit has two blue or black stripes along the sides. In ancient times one of the fringes in each corner would be dyed dark blue. Today no one knows how to make this dye which came from a shellfish, so the fringes are all white. The stripes remind Jews of the dark blue dye.

TEFILLIN (SINGULAR TEFILLAH)

Jewish males over the age of thirteen wear tefillin at morning prayer each day except Shabbat and festivals. Boys start to practise putting them on a few weeks before their **bar mitzvah**.

Tefillin are two leather boxes, one worn on the upper arm, the other on the head. Inside

FACTFILE

More about tefillin

What really matters is what is going on inside a person's mind. It is important to develop pure thoughts. The purpose of the tefillin is to direct the wearer's thoughts to God. Maimonides, the Jewish philosopher, wrote, '…so long as the tefillin are on the head and arm of a man, he is humble and God-fearing, he turns his heart exclusively to words of truth and justice.' The straps are wound around the hand to form the letter 'shin', which stands for 'Shadai' – one of the names of God.

'And these matters which I command you today you shall take to heart. And you shall teach them carefully to your children and you shall speak of them…'

(Deuteronomy 6:6–7)

Education for the Jew is a life-long process that continues into old age.

JEWISH EDUCATION IN THE PAST

Jewish parents have always tried to make sure that their children grew up knowing how a Jew should live. They taught them in their homes, by personal example (see page 64). On **Shabbat** and **Rosh Chodesh** (New Moon) people of both sexes used to gather in the Temple court to listen to priests and prophets (*II Kings 4:23*).

In the first century CE Joshua ben Gamla, a High Priest, set up schools in the Holy Land. He made the communities pay the teachers' wages. In the Middle Ages, wealthy parents employed tutors for their sons. The poor still went to community schools. Boys could progress to higher education in Talmudic academies, or **yeshivot** (singular **yeshiva**). Old men studied in synagogues and were joined by young men after their day's work was over. There was no similar provision for girls.

Jewish education for girls really began in the nineteenth century. In Germany and Poland, schools and seminaries were set up where girls could study Hebrew, the Bible, **Shulchan Aruch** (see page 32) and Jewish history (see Unit 44).

JEWISH EDUCATION IN BRITAIN

Early in the twentieth century there were a few Jewish schools for the children of refugees (see page 12) from eastern Europe. By World War I these schools began to close. Instead, the children attended classes called **Talmud Torah** in the synagogues after school and on Sunday mornings. They learned Hebrew and basic Jewish subjects. However, during the 1920s and 1930s many Jews began to desert their religion. For example, a Talmud Torah teacher who tried to tell his pupils they should not travel on Shabbat (see page 41) would achieve little when parents were taking the children to football matches on Saturday afternoons.

The **Holocaust** (see page 16) and the founding of the State of Israel in 1948 (see page 13) marked a turning point for Jewish education in Britain. British Jews began to feel that their Jewish identity mattered. There was also more money available to build new schools. Today there are about 40 Jewish nursery schools, 30 primary schools and 20 secondary schools and two schools for Jewish children with disabilities. There are 45 000 Jewish children in Britain: 30 per cent are in Jewish schools. Others attend **cheder**, part-time classes similar to the old Talmud Torah.

Jewish schools provide time for Jewish studies. Nursery and primary school children have Jewish songs and stories. They act out Shabbat and festival customs. In secondary school they study the Bible, Talmud and Shulchan Aruch. Girls may prepare for seminary (see Unit 44) and boys for yeshiva.

Jewish secondary schools include the full range of GCSE and A level choices and they

Acting out Shabbat in a Jewish nursery (see photograph on page 37)

usually include Biblical or Modern Hebrew (or both).

HIGHER EDUCATION

Jews who leave school may start work or go to college or university. Those who want higher Jewish education can attend yeshiva (boys) or seminary (for girls and women, see Unit 44).

YESHIVA

Yeshiva is not like college or university, as there is no set course to follow, nor is there a written diploma at the end. Boys usually begin at sixteen and study parts of the Talmud (see page 31), the Bible, Shulchan Aruch, Jewish philosophy and **Midrashim** (see page 33). There are oral examinations to decide when they are ready to progress to a higher level of study.

Students prepare for lectures and learn in a **chavruta** (paired learning). Those who have completed all the classes study in chavruta all the time. They only need to consult the lecturers over particularly difficult points. A yeshiva study hall is a lively, noisy place as so much learning is by discussion, argument and questioning. Each boy learns to block out other voices and only hear his **chaver** (partner). They study for long hours, starting before morning prayers and going on until after 9 p.m.

Few boys who go to yeshiva want to become **rabbis**, they simply want to learn more about their religion. If they want to become a rabbi they take a special course that takes many years (see page 93). Boys may attend yeshiva for any period, from one to five years.

ADULT EDUCATION

Most synagogues run courses for adults of both sexes and some offer a wide range of subjects. Study of the Bible or Talmud involves discussions and lectures. There is a large range of books about Jewish topics, many in English.

Jewish devotion to learning made Jews a very literate group, when many people in Europe could neither read nor write. Today, all the most modern learning media are used, such as interactive videos and computers.

FACTFILE

Youth Aliya

Youth Aliya was founded in 1933 to rescue Jewish young people from Nazi Germany. About 5000 teenagers were taken to Israel before World War II and educated in Youth Aliya boarding schools. After the war another 15 000 youngsters joined them, most of them Holocaust survivors. Today Youth Aliya villages have about 14 000 pupils, including disadvantaged young Israelis who need a second chance.

REFLECTION

'The chavruta system is very challenging because it's not possible to switch off in the way I've done in countless lectures and sessions of private study.'

(Mr B, North London)

POINT OF VIEW

Many Jews fear that the problems that affected the Talmud Torah system are still there and many Jewish children in Britain receive little Jewish education.

WOMEN AND MITZVOT

In the past Jewish women rarely took part in public activities or became leaders. Judaism taught that the role of wife and mother were important aspects of a woman's development (see page 76).

Today, there have been great changes in opportunities for women in education and the world of work. Religious Jews welcome these new opportunities for women. However, they reject the idea that marriage and motherhood are a burden and somehow second-best to a career. For Jews, raising and caring for children is a privilege, not an unjust demand.

They regard the woman's role as so important that the **halakhah** (see page 30) frees women from many religious mitzvot (tasks and obligations). They do not even have to pray together with the community at set times. Many women do carry out these mitzvot and attend communal prayers, but they do so from personal choice, and not from obligation.

EDUCATION FOR WOMEN

Until the eighteenth century Judaism did not make much provision for education for girls and women. Most girls learned their Judaism at home, by watching and listening. Some wealthy parents hired tutors for their daughters, but the range of subjects was limited. However, there have been some outstanding female Talmudic scholars. For example, Bruria in the second century CE was consulted by the **rabbis** of her day. The wife of a sixteenth-century rabbi was so learned that she gave halakhic advice to the congregation when her husband was absent.

The first schools for Jewish girls were set up in Germany by **maskilim** in the eighteenth century (see page 10). Girls learnt German, Hebrew, arithmetic, art and craft and some Jewish studies. However the aim of the maskilim was to get Jews to merge into society and their schools were often very like ordinary non-Jewish schools. The first person to open a secondary school for girls that was committed to Jewish education was Rabbi Sampson Raphael Hirsch (see page 132).

SARAH SCHENEIRER (1883–1935)

Women in Eastern Europe were denied this opportunity. Sarah Scheneirer of Cracow, Poland, realised that without religious education, Jewish women were likely to follow the worldly way of life of the time. In 1918 she began teaching a group of teenage girls. When they had a grasp of some basic Jewish subjects, they went out to teach others. In this way she spread Jewish education for women. She was a dedicated and inspiring teacher. By the 1930s there were hundreds of schools providing for over 80 000 Jewish girls. Her movement was known as Bet Yaakov (House of Jacob). Today there are schools and seminaries for Jewish girls all over the world.

◇

A science lesson in a Jewish girls' school

GIRLS' SEMINARY

Girls study a wider range of subjects in seminary than the boys do at **yeshiva** (see page 89). The courses are also more structured. There is usually a three-year course, but many students only stay for one or two years. There are examinations and diplomas at the end of the courses. Most girls start seminary after GCSE or A levels, but some seminaries run courses for women in their 20s and 30s.

Subjects include Hebrew, Bible, **Midrash**, Jewish literature, Jewish history, philosophy and **Shulchan Aruch**. There are vocational courses, including teacher training and secretarial skills. Teaching methods are similar to those at college and university, with lectures, essays and research projects. The **chavruta** system of the yeshiva is also used.

SYNAGOGUE STUDIES

Many synagogues offer a variety of subjects for women at all grades. In the USA and Israel women can study to a very high level at evening classes or on short residential courses. Some courses are aimed at older women, and some attract university graduates.

WOMEN IN THE SYNAGOGUE

Women can pray wherever they choose and are not tied to the set times of prayer. Men, however, must pray together at fixed times. This is why a **minyan**, the ten worshippers needed for communal prayer, must be men (but see page 143). Ten is the lowest number regarded as a communal unit. Women who choose to join in communal prayer have a separate area in which to pray. However, only men will conduct the service, read from the **Torah** scroll (see page 85) and be called up to say a blessing over the reading (see page 38).

There has recently been a strong movement among women who feel they want to take a more active part in prayer. The first women's prayer group was formed in a synagogue in London in 1992. The group held its prayer sessions in a room in the synagogue at the same time as the main service. Some rabbis wanted the women to stay with the minyan for the set prayers. The Chief Rabbi therefore ruled that women's prayer groups could not meet on synagogue premises at the same time as the main service. The number of women's prayer groups is increasing and women are being elected to synagogue management boards.

FACTFILE

Women – past and present

In Biblical times special provision was made for the rights of women. In the Creation story woman is described as an equally valuable partner to man. Man and woman were created equally in the image of God, and together were called 'man' and formed a single unit. This led to the rabbinic statement that whoever 'is not married is not a man'.

The founders of the Jews include Matriarchs as well as the Patriarchs. Miriam, Deborah, Hannah, Ruth and Esther are among many Biblical heroines.

In theory, women may become **shochet** or **mohel**, but rarely do in practice. However, there are growing numbers of women teaching in Jewish colleges. In Reform seminaries many women are studying to become rabbis.

'All who occupy themselves with the affairs of the community should do so for the sake of Heaven.'

(Ethics of the Fathers)

Jewish communities employ many people to provide their members with a range of services. There are also volunteers who give their services free to the community.

THE RABBI

Rabbi is a Hebrew word that means 'my master' or 'sir'. This is the title of the religious leader of a Jewish community (see page 25).

Rabbis in the past

In ancient times rabbis earned their living doing ordinary jobs such as carpenters, farmers and blacksmiths. The rabbis were wise and holy men. People could turn to them for guidance on many issues, but mainly on questions of Jewish law. They also gave public lectures.

These rabbis had groups of followers or disciples, who then went on to be rabbis themselves. The most learned of them lectured in the **yeshivot** (Talmudic academies, see page 89). If they were asked to judge in a dispute, they would form a **bet din**, a rabbinical court, with two other rabbis,.

In the fourteenth century the Black Death wiped out nearly a quarter of the population of Europe. The Jews were blamed for this plague, and many were murdered. After the plague ended, Jewish communities began to be built up once more. The leaders decided to offer salaries to rabbis so that they could devote their whole time to the community. At about the same time some rabbis began to give diplomas to their best students. These stated that they had a high standard of learning and a good character. The diplomas are still issued to rabbis today.

Rabbis today

A modern rabbi has many tasks to perform. He sometimes leads prayers or reads the weekly **sidra** (**Torah** portion, see page 38). He conducts weddings and funerals. He is very much involved in Jewish education and conducts study sessions, particularly on **Shabbat**.

A rabbi also has a pastoral role, caring for the members of his community. He may be the Jewish chaplain to a local hospital or prison. He will care for Jewish university students. Some rabbis are marriage guidance counsellors.

In traditional communities rabbis spend most time studying, teaching or deciding matters of Jewish law (see the picture below).

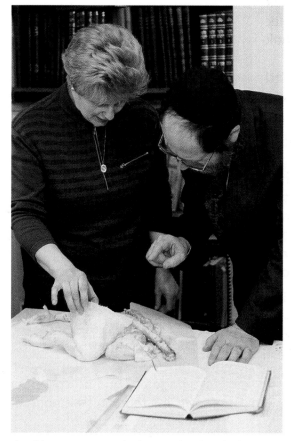

*A rabbi examines a chicken to decide whether it is **kosher***

TRAINING TO BE A RABBI

A rabbi must know about Jewish law, in particular **kashrut** (laws about food, see page 68). He must also know about the observance of Shabbat and festivals, and marriage and mourning customs. Students only begin training to become rabbis after several years of general Biblical and Talmudic studies.

Students who become rabbis must have a good character. Some rabbis also have a degree in Jewish studies. Some may spend several years at a **kollel**, an institute of higher learning for rabbis, before taking up their post.

Today, some rabbis specialize in certain areas of **halakhah** (see page 32), such as medical issues concerning abortion, euthanasia and organ transplant. Others specialize in halakhic questions concerning the use of electronics on Shabbat and festivals, or in halakhot regarding business and commerce.

THE CHAZAN

A **chazan** (cantor) is a man chosen for his fine voice. His role is to lead the congregation in prayer. He chants (sings) parts of the prayers on Shabbat and festivals. He usually leads the service alone, but some synagogues have choirs to help him. He often assists the rabbi at weddings, funerals and memorial services. Those synagogues who do not have a chazan appoint members of the congregation to lead the prayers.

The chazan has special training in music and voice projection. He has to learn the various chants (musical settings) for different festivals. Some chazanim (plural of chazan) attend yeshiva, but most have no rabbinic training. The chazan may also sing Jewish songs at weddings or other celebrations.

FACTFILE 1

One of the greatest rabbis

Many Jews regard Rabbi Moses ben Maimon (1135–1204 CE, usually known as Maimonides) as one of the greatest rabbis.

He was a brilliant scholar and physician. Before he was 25 years old he became chief rabbi of Cairo and physician to Saladin, sultan of Egypt and Syria.

His contribution to the development of Judaism earned him the title 'second Moses'. His greatest work is the **Mishnah Torah**, set out in 14 books and written in Hebrew (1170–80). He also wrote the Thirteen Articles of Faith, to which many Orthodox Jews still adhere.

He was also a philosopher, and in *Guide for the Perplexed*, written in Arabic in c.1190 CE, Maimonides tried to bring together Jewish faith and his Greek philosophy. In this book he wrote about the nature of God and creation, free will, and the problem of good and evil.

FACTFILE 2

Rabbinical seminaries

In the USA there are new kinds of rabbinical seminary. The largest are the Yeshiva University (Orthodox) and the Jewish Theological Seminary (Conservative), both in New York, and the Hebrew Union College-Jewish Institute of Religion (Reform) in Cincinnati, Ohio.

THE GABBAI

A **gabbai** is a synagogue warden. He is responsible for the way that services in the synagogue are run. He chooses people to lead the prayers that the **chazan** does not chant. He asks people to open or close the Ark (see page 84) or to take out the **Torah** scrolls. The gabbai also calls people to read the Torah. At the end of **Shabbat** morning prayers the gabbai tells the congregation the times of future services and special events.

THE SHAMASH

The gabbai's assistant is called the **shamash** (servant). He makes sure that people have **siddurim** (prayer books) and **tallitot** (prayer robes). Most people have their own, but the synagogue keeps spares for anyone who does not. The shamash also ensures that there is wine for **kiddush** (see page 37) or **havdalah** (see page 39). He sees that books are put away at the end of the service.

OTHER SYNAGOGUE WORKERS

The synagogue needs a caretaker to keep it clean, make sure the heating is turned on and carry out minor repairs. Caretakers sometimes live in a house or flat provided by the community. In addition, a board of officers may be elected to manage the synagogue and its finances. Larger synagogues may have several groups running its activities. These officers and groups are volunteers.

THE SOFER (SCRIBE)

'One should not live in a town that has no **sofer**.'

(Talmud)

Soferim (plural of sofer) write the Torah scrolls used in the synagogue (see page 85). They also write the small scrolls that go into **tefillin** (see page 87) and **mezuzot** (see page 66). They also check and repair them.

A sofer also writes the **get** (document of divorce). Soferim have very responsible jobs.

A sofer will first study at **yeshiva** (see page 89) for several years. Then he becomes an apprentice to a qualified sofer. The sofer teaches him how to prepare parchment from animal skins, how to make ink and to cut quill or reed pens. It takes a long time to perfect the Hebrew lettering, and to learn the different styles of the **Ashkenazi** and **Sephardi** Jews.

He has to learn how to open tefillin for inspection and sew them up again. He may learn to make the tefillin. He also learns how to repair Torah scrolls for synagogues.

When the apprentice is good enough, he takes an examination in scribal law. His master writes him a certificate of competence and now he can work as a sofer in his own right.

The community relies on the sofer to ensure that their mezuzot and tefillin are **kosher** (for example, see page 67). He must be a person of such integrity that his word is beyond doubt.

THE SHOCHET

A **shochet** is a butcher who slaughters (kills) animals for food. He must make sure that meat is kosher (see page 68).

Like the sofer, the shochet begins his training after several years at yeshiva. He too must become an apprentice. He studies the laws of **shechitah**, Jewish method of slaughter (see page 68) and watches expert slaughterers at work. He learns to take care of the shechitah knife.

The trainee studies the bodies of animals and birds, so that he can inspect carcasses for defects. If internal organs are missing, deformed or diseased a carcass is **treifah** (not kosher, see page 68). The shochet must be able to recognize these faults.

A sofer (scribe) writing part of a Torah scroll

He begins by slaughtering poultry – and may choose to remain a shochet of poultry. The shechitah of animals is more difficult. When he reaches the right standard, he receives a certificate allowing him to practise shechitah. He must be deeply religious. He is the only one who knows whether he killed an animal properly. His word must be beyond doubt.

THE MOHEL

The **mohel** is responsible for circumcising Jewish males. His work and training are described on page 73.

◇

FACTFILE

Origins of gabbai and shamash

The word gabbai means 'collector'. In earlier times charity collectors were held in high esteem. Their honesty was beyond question. However, the Talmud advises that, to avoid suspicion, charity collectors should work in pairs.

Shamash is also the name given to the ninth candle used during **hanukkah** (see page 57) to light the eight candles of the festival.

MIKVEH ATTENDANTS

As part of family purity Jewish women visit the **mikveh** after a period or after childbirth (see page 77). A mikveh attendant, usually an older woman, is there to make sure that each woman prepares properly before she immerses. The attendant stands at the edge to see that the woman immerses totally. Sometimes a woman's hair may float on the surface. The attendant watches out for this, and helps to make sure the immersion is complete.

Mikveh attendants have to know all the laws about immersion, and must be kind and understanding, especially with brides and young wives.

SHATNEZ TESTING

The **Torah** forbids Jews to wear **shatnez**, wool and linen fibres, in the same garment. (*Deuteronomy 22:11*, see page 64).

The ban on the wearing of shatnez is one of the **chukim** (see page 22). This means no reason is given for it. Keeping this law is an act of faith. Special laboratories test clothing for observant Jews. There are testing facilities in London, Manchester and Gateshead. Shatnez may be in the form of linen stiffening or stitching in woollen garments. If this happens, the suit or coat will be taken to a Jewish tailor who replaces the linen inserts with a different fabric.

Fibres as seen through the microscope

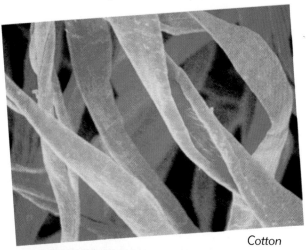

Cotton

Wool

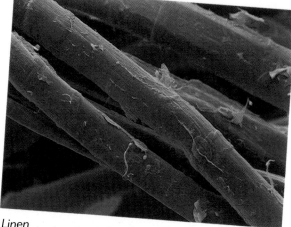

Linen

Silk

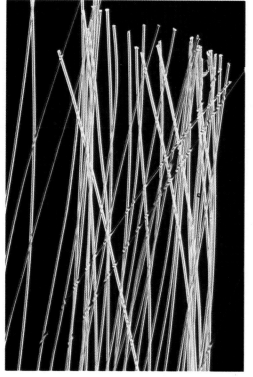

Nylon

THE BET DIN (RABBINICAL COURT)

A **bet din** is a panel of judges who listen to people putting their case in Jewish law. They question witnesses and reach a verdict before giving their decision.

In ancient Israel there were three kinds of bet din. Ordinary cases were heard by three judges. For crimes which carried a death penalty, 23 judges presided. If more than one person's life was at stake, for example in a war, there was a supreme court of 71 judges. This was called the **Sanhedrin**. No Jewish court has carried out a death sentence since Roman times. Today there is only the bet din of three judges.

The judges (**dayanim**) are usually experienced **rabbis**. Sometimes Jews take business disputes to a bet din. Most rabbinical courts today, however, are concerned with divorces, conversions and decisions about food products.

THE CHEVRA KADDISHA (BURIAL SOCIETY)

Chevra kaddisha means 'holy society'. It is a group of men and women who prepare bodies for burial. Jews regard burying the dead as a holy responsibility. It is the 'true kindness' since the one receiving the kindness cannot repay it. Jews think of the body as a garment which a soul needs in order to carry out **mitzvot** (see page 22). For this reason a body is treated with great respect.

The chevra kaddisha must know the laws about preparing bodies. A Jewish body must not be made up with cosmetics nor dressed and laid out in a fancy casket. Instead, members of the chevra kaddisha wash it, wrap it in a plain linen shroud and place it in a plain wooden coffin.

SUPPLIERS OF KOSHER FOOD

Jews are only allowed to eat **kosher** food (see page 68) so it is important that they have shops that sell it. In Jewish areas supermarkets often have a kosher section. Shopkeepers do not need a licence to sell kosher food, as the food products themselves have a **hechsher** (seal of kashrut) on them (see page 70). Jewish butchers, bakers and restaurants do need a licence from a bet din because they prepare the food themselves.

FACTFILE

Kosher cooking

The observance of kashrut (the Jewish dietary laws) has resulted in the development of a distinctively 'Jewish' style of cooking. The recipes included in Units 18, 24, 25 and 34 are examples of this. You may like to try one of them.

'...what the Lord requires of you is to do justice and loving kindness and to walk humbly with your God.'

(Micah 6:8)

Some Jewish rules are set down in clear terms. This is what the **Shulchan Aruch** does (see page 32). With moral principles it is not so easy. The **Torah** gives guidance for moral behaviour. However, individuals have to decide for themselves exactly how they are going to apply the guidelines.

For example, should we always tell the truth even if it means someone gets hurt? (see page 100). How should we combine justice and kindness when dealing with a criminal? There cannot be clear-cut rules for every situation. The way an individual reaches a decision depends on how he or she feels about a particular problem. It also depends on the kind of person they are and whether they have developed a moral sense. Judaism has something to say about the development of moral sensitivity.

MORALITY AND HOLINESS

For the Jew, true holiness is found in both caring for other people and observing the **mitzvot**. For this reason, they have no time for monks or hermits. These are people who withdraw from human company to concentrate on their spiritual lives. Neither do they accept the idea of caring for people purely from humanitarian concern. If people claim to be moral without the 'spiritual dimension' then an important element is missing from their morality.

The **Mishnah** says, 'On three things the world stands: on the study of the Torah, on worship and on deeds of kindness.'

These ideas are very ancient. On page 6 we saw that the Patriarchs of the Jews combined worship of God with hospitality to others. The Ten Commandments show that right living is

Learning to share

part of serving God. The Prophet Isaiah reminded people that if they wanted God to hear their prayers they would have to 'seek justice, relieve the oppressed, treat the orphan justly and help the widow' (*Isaiah 1:17*).

MITZVOT AND PERSONAL DEVELOPMENT

Page 22 explains that keeping the mizvot leads to character-building. People generally understand that the way we think and feel affects the way we behave. Jewish principles turn this around – the way we behave affects the way we think. Morality is not simply a question of keeping rules. However, observing mitzvot daily until they become second nature affects the way people develop as individuals.

ETHICAL MITZVOT

These are the mitzvot that are 'between one person and another'. They include respecting parents, helping the poor, being careful not to steal – like not keeping extra change a shopkeeper has given. Keeping these mitzvot help a person to develop morally.

'BETWEEN A PERSON AND GOD'

The mitzvot that are 'between a person and God' include regular prayers and observance of holy days. These also shape a person's moral character. For example, the Jewish prayers remind people of the needs of others. The **Shabbat**, with its ban on work, enables Jews to spend more time with the family. **Pesach** is a time to think about freedom. The Day of Atonement is for thinking about forgiveness. **Purim** reminds Jews of the problems faced by those who live under cruel, tyrannical governments.

Even remembering the destruction of the Jerusalem Temple in 70 CE is an opportunity to think about other people's needs. Jews believe that the coming of the Messiah (see page 24) might be brought nearer by acts of love and kindness towards other people. The Temple would be rebuilt at this time.

THE MORAL INDIVIDUAL

A moral individual is someone who combines religious observance with concern for other people. It is someone who sees moral behaviour as an essential part of serving God.

FACTFILE 1

The prophets
Isaiah, Jeremiah, Hosea and Micah are prophets who preached about morality.

FACTFILE 2

The Spirit of Goodness
(From a story by David Kossoff.)

Rabbi Mark decided to preach a sermon about people who exploited their workers.

'There was once an upright, strict man who lived in a fine house and ran a big business. Every Sabbath he worshipped and on all the High Days and Holy Days he fasted and he feasted. He had an old servant called Pertchick who did far too much for the small wage he was paid. Pertchick's wife became ill and needed medicines and good food to eat. Pertchick knew his employer wouldn't help so he started to steal from him. God saw this and sent the Spirit of Goodness to see him.

Pertchick explained to the Spirit that such stealing was essential. Goodness asked how he could help. 'Perhaps if you went to my employer and explained – he might give me a little more money, a house not so damp…'

'I would,' said Goodness, 'but he does not know of me. I've called on him a number of times but I'm a stranger to him. You see, some people, even thieves like yourself, know me straight away. Others, even strictly observing and regularly worshipping people – to them I'm invisible. They seem to think they can do better without Goodness.'

Even a thief can recognize Goodness, while others do not seem to understand that what they're doing is immoral.

'O my God, guard my tongue from evil and my lips from speaking deceitfully.'

(Prayer Book)

The **Midrash** tells this story:

One day a man told his servant to go and buy the best meat in the market. The servant brought back a tongue. The next day he sent him to buy the worst thing in the market. Again the servant brought a tongue. When he asked the servant to explain his choices, he replied, 'Nothing is better than a good tongue, and nothing is worse than a bad one.'

Judaism stresses the importance of words. Jews are expected to tell the truth, not to humiliate or mislead people, nor spread

You never know who's listening!

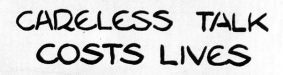

CARELESS TALK COSTS LIVES

This World War II poster is about the power of the spoken word

rumours. This applies to both the written and spoken word.

TRUTH AND FALSEHOOD

The **Torah** tells Jews to 'Keep far away from a false word' (*Exodus 23:7*) and, 'That which goes out of your lips you shall keep and do' (*Deuteronomy 23:24*). The **Talmud** calls truth God's seal.

However, teaching about truth and falsehood is not always simple. Sometimes it is better to keep some of the truth back. For example, Jews disapprove of boasting. The Talmud allows people to hold back the truth when questioned about their achievements.

There may be times when a lie is allowed. For example, Elisha, a Prophet, was asked by a sick Aramean king whether he would recover. Elisha could see he was going to die but to have said so would have been cruel. So he told the king's messenger to say to him, 'You shall certainly live' (*II Kings 8:7–15*).

Similarly, during the **Holocaust** (see page 16) people risked their lives to hide Jews. They knew that by lying to the German soldiers they were doing the right thing.

DECEPTION

Advertising often tells the truth in such a way that it implies something that is not true. A manufacturer of washing-up liquid may say, 'This product contains no nitrates' to make it sound more eco-friendly. But detergents do not contain nitrates in any case. The Talmud calls this deception and it is forbidden in Judaism.

THE WHOLE TRUTH

In some cases the slightest departure from the truth – or even an honest mistake – becomes a sin. In court, witnesses are asked to make statements under oath (swearing on the name of God or a holy object). Many Jews choose to affirm they will tell the whole truth in a court of law rather than swear to it. This is because they take the truth very seriously, and realize that memory can be faulty, and they may make a mistake in their testimony.

SPREADING RUMOURS

'Do not go about as tale-bearers.'

(Leviticus 19:16)

It is a serious offence for a Jew to pass on unpleasant information about another person. The Torah forbids this, even if the information is true. People can slip into this kind of talk – gossip – without thinking. On the other hand, it is not clear cut. Sometimes it may be necessary and allowed to pass on unpleasant information. For example, it would be right to warn a shopkeeper that a dishonest person is passing dud cheques.

CAUSING EMBARRASSMENT

'Someone who humiliates another person in public has no share in the World to Come.'

(Ethics of the Fathers)

The Talmud says, 'You can kill a person only once, but when you humiliate him, you kill him many times over.' People who feel humiliated by someone else's unkind words may feel uncomfortable or ashamed whenever they think about it.

KEY WORDS

Libel – writing or broadcasting damaging untruths about someone

Slander – passing on such information by word of mouth

FACTFILE

The naked truth...?

The Midrash tells the following story.

One day Truth came into the world. She went to a big city expecting to be greeted with joy, but instead everyone turned their backs on her. In every city, people didn't want to know her. Saddened, Truth left the towns and sat down by the roadside. Along came Parable and asked her why she was crying. Truth told him what had happened. 'I just don't understand why people turn away from me,' she cried. 'But just look at you,' said Parable. 'You are naked. That's why no one wants to know you. Come, I will clothe you.' So Parable dressed Truth up and wherever she went people accepted her.

The meaning of this story is that sometimes the plain truth can be hard to accept. It may be painful to hear, so it has to be 'softened' by careful choice of words.

Sometimes truth can be hard to explain. This is specially so with religious statements. When a religious person tries to explain an important matter, then often parables or illustrations are used. Some people think the story of Creation in Genesis is like this. It says that God created the world and all that is in it, and why He did so. It is not meant to be read as a scientific explanation.

'Not to have known suffering is not to be truly human.'

(Midrash)

People who believe that God is good, all-powerful and ever-present (see page 18) ask – why do innocent people suffer? Why does a child have an incurable illness? Jews today ask about the **Holocaust** (see page 16), 'Where was God in the concentration camps?'

There are no simple answers to questions about suffering. Only the prophets (see page 7) who were close to God were told the reasons for particular disasters. The **rabbis** could not give reasons for suffering, but they found ways of approaching it. These were often based on stories in the **Tenakh**.

SUFFERING IN THE TENAKH

The Tenakh describes how people coped with suffering and came through. Joseph was sold as a slave by his brothers (*Genesis 37:28*). Ruth was a young widow and very poor (*Ruth 1:2–5*). King David's baby son died

(*II Samuel 12:1–18*). The book of *Job* is all about suffering. It is about a man who lost his home and family, and endured terrible pain, yet never once turned against God (see page 28).

Stories like these help people to accept suffering. Suffering may be a punishment sent by God, a test of faith or a reminder to people of their promise of loyalty to God. There may be other reasons. The main points are (a) suffering does not 'just happen' – God makes it happen, and (b) as suffering comes from God there must be a reason for it.

TEACHINGS OF THE RABBIS

The rabbis of the **Talmud** and **Midrash** never tried to justify suffering. They never said it was right or fair. They did try to show that some good can come from it. They taught that suffering might be a call to repent. It shows people they are responsible for one another. Sometimes good people suffer for the sake of the wicked. They said that God never tests people beyond what they can endure. They also said that suffering can

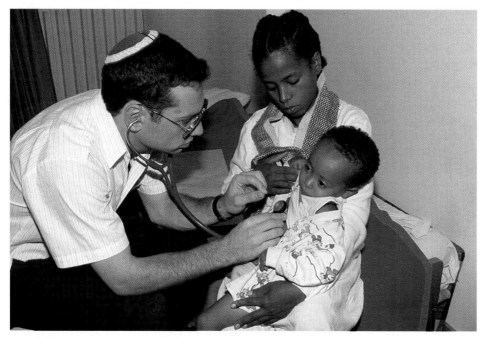

Jews believe it is important to relieve suffering

refine people's characters by teaching them to be patient, humble and sensitive to the pain of others. It helps to remind them how short life is and to be aware of its purpose. In addition, people can come through suffering stronger than they were before. They are better people as a result.

JEWISH PHILOSOPHY

A different – and difficult – idea is put forward by Jewish philosophers. They felt suffering was necessary so that people could be free to choose between good and evil (see page 20). If God only gave us good things, then we would have no choice but to love him. We would be obliged to do good. Suffering makes it possible for people to reject God and do evil.

RELIEF OF SUFFERING

The Talmud gives good advice about avoiding illness and unnecessary suffering. The rabbis also taught that every effort should be made to relieve suffering. It is a religious duty to visit the sick, provide for the poor and comfort the bereaved. There have always been Jewish organizations providing for those in need (see page 118).

Laughter – the best medicine

The Talmud tells of a rabbi who wanted to see someone who had earned a place in heaven. He was shown two men in the market place. He asked, 'What is your job?' They replied, 'We are clowns; we try to lift people out of their sadness.'

EUTHANASIA

According to Jewish thinking, killing people to put them out of their misery is murder. It is murder even if they ask for it. However, Jews would not allow people to continue to suffer. They would not allow active euthanasia (mercy killing) but they would allow withholding treatment from someone who is

beyond help. Switching off a life-support machine would be murder if there was even the slightest chance that the patient might recover. If there is no longer any heart, brain or lung activity, the machine could be turned off. It would be no longer *supporting* life – it is *providing* it.

FACTFILE

More about euthanasia

Euthanasia comes from a Greek word meaning an 'easy death'. In human terms it refers to mercy killing – the practice of ending a life to save a person from unbearable suffering when they have an incurable and painful disease. Voluntary euthanasia is when the sick person asks to be allowed to die or to be helped to die.

Active euthanasia involves someone taking deliberate action to cause a death. In Britain it is illegal for anyone to help someone to die.

Passive euthanasia means *not* doing something to prevent death. This may be withholding life-saving medicine or not resuscitating someone after a heart attack or stroke.

Modern machines can keep someone alive even when they are permanently unconscious. Some people think that carrying life on in this way is unkind to both the patient and the patient's family.

POINT OF VIEW

Judaism teaches that life is God's creation and therefore belongs to Him. Humans do not have the right to take away what God has given.

'Keeping the body fit and healthy is part of serving God…a person should avoid whatever undermines bodily health.'

(Maimonides)

For the Jew, keeping the body clean and healthy is a religious duty.

CLEANLINESS

The **Talmud** (see page 31) tells the story of **Hillel**, a first-century **rabbi**, who told his students he was going to the bath-house to carry out an important **mitzvah** (see page 22). He explained, 'See how the statues of kings are scrubbed and kept clean by specially appointed officials. Should not we, who are created in the image of God (*Genesis 1:27*), have even greater regard for the cleanliness of our bodies?'

'A person must wash his face, hands and feet each day in honour of his Creator.'

(Talmud)

The Talmud also teaches Jews to rinse their mouths before praying in the morning and to wash their hands before meals and after using the lavatory. These are religious duties. However, there are healthy results. During the Great Plague of 1665 when hundreds of people died, hardly any Jews became ill.

HEALTH

The Talmud contains sound advice for healthy living. It advises people to sleep and eat at regular times, but not to excess. It tells them not to sit, stand or walk for too long. It also shows the link between physical, mental and spiritual health. 'Three things drain a person's health: worry, travel and sin.'

The Talmud warns people not to do things that could be dangerous, such as entering a ruined building, walking across a rickety bridge or drinking from a stream at night when you cannot see what you are drinking.

'Wine enters, sense goes out; wine enters, secrets come out' (Midrash)

There are three habits today that people know to be harmful:

- drinking alcohol
- taking drugs
- smoking tobacco.

Alcohol

Jews are allowed to drink alcohol. They use wine in religious ceremonies (see pages 37 and 39). However, Jews strongly disapprove of drinking alcohol in large quantities. The **Midrash** says, 'Wine enters, sense goes out; wine enters, secrets come out.'

For Jews with certain jobs even a small amount of alcohol is not allowed. For example, a judge who drank even one glass of wine would be considered unfit to pass judgement until a suitable time had passed.

Today we know that too much alcohol can cause brain damage and liver damage. Many Jews think alcohol abuse is similar to the harmful practices that the Talmud forbids.

Drugs

Some young Jews are becoming addicted to drugs, though not generally in religious families. There are drug counselling services (see page 119) in some Jewish care organizations.

Some synagogues believe that education about the risks of drugs should form part of their religion classes.

There are three **halakhot** (see page 30) about alcohol and drug abuse.

- Jews are forbidden to break the laws of the country in which they live. Most countries have laws against drunkenness and drug abuse/peddling.

- Alcohol and drug abuse lead to loss of self-control and inability to follow God's commands.

- Jews believe a person does not own his own body and therefore must not cause damage to it. The body is God's creation (*Genesis 2:7*) and must be treated with respect. This applies to smoking tobacco as well.

Tobacco

Since it became known that smoking tobacco is a major cause of lung and heart disease, many Jews have come to think of it as against their religious teachings. Today, it is also known that 'passive smoking' (breathing other people's smoke) is harmful. In 1982, Rabbi Eliezer Waldenberg, an authority on these matters, wrote:

> 'There are sufficient grounds to forbid smoking according to the Torah. Similarly, when someone is smoking in a public place, [others] have a right to object.'

More Jews are now against smoking and discourage children from smoking. Some synagogues have non-smoking areas.

SUICIDE

For the Jew, God gives life and only God can take it away (*Deuteronomy 32:39*). Suicide is a serious sin and a Jew who commits suicide is buried in a separate part of the cemetery.

However, this would not be the case if the person was mentally ill at the time.

FACTFILE 1

You are what you eat!

People in Britain, as in America, are getting fatter. Despite the fashion for health and fitness, obesity (being too fat) is a cause of concern. In the past ten years the percentage of people who are obese has doubled. Thirty-two per cent of all adults are overweight. On top of this another thirteen per cent of men and sixteen per cent of women are excessively overweight.

Eating habits have greatly changed in the last twenty years. There is a huge increase in the amount of fatty foods being eaten (bad news). The consumption of chips has more than doubled, and the amount of crisps eaten has increased six times.

FACTFILE 2

Permitted killing

Judaism only gives people the right to take a life in self-defence, war, or when a court of law passes a death sentence.

'If men fight and one injures the other…[the attacker] must make sure that [the injured man] is completely healed (*Exodus 21:19*). From here we see that it is right for physicians to heal.'

(Talmud)

In the **Torah** God says, 'I, the Lord, am your healer' (*Exodus 15:26*). In their morning prayers Jews praise God as 'the healer of all flesh'. Judaism teaches that we should not rely on miracles, so they see doctors as the agents through whom God heals the sick.

There have always been ethical questions concerning medicine. For example, whether it was right to run away from a town where there was plague, or whether a Jew should eat non-**kosher** food if a doctor prescribed it as a cure. Modern medicine raises more difficult questions, some of which are set out in this unit.

AUTOPSIES

Autopsies (examinations carried out on dead bodies) raise several **halakhic** problems. Jews are not permitted to mutilate (cut up) a corpse, make money from it, nor delay burial. The principle of preserving life, however, comes first. **Rabbi** Yechezial Landau (1713–1793) said it was right to perform an autopsy if it would help to find a cure for another patient who was 'near at hand'. Today, with modern forms of travel and communication, rabbis think 'near at hand' includes anywhere in the world.

Rabbis also permit an autopsy on anyone who dies from a rare disease (if the patient agreed to it previously). This allows other patients to benefit from the information gained. If the patient did not give consent before they died, a group of rabbis can authorize the autopsy if the patient's family has given consent. Sometimes the coroner asks for an autopsy. When an autopsy has to be carried out by law, Jews obey the law.

ORGAN TRANSPLANTS

There are two kinds of organ transplants: those from a living donor and those from a dead one.

Someone may wish to donate a kidney to someone else. The question is whether it is right to risk one's own life to save another. Most rabbis would agree to this provided the donor is in good health and has consented to give the organ. No one should be forced to donate an organ.

The same rules that are set out for autopsies apply to removing an organ from a dead donor. If it is to save a life, rabbis would usually agree. Even eye transplants, they say, come into this category. A blind person is always at risk of a life-threatening accident.

The most serious problem concerns heart transplants. A heart must be removed as soon as possible after the donor is dead. But however desperately the recipient needs the organ, no one may kill (murder) one patient to save the life of another.

◇

ABORTION

Jews object to abortion. They believe it destroys a potential life.

However, Jews will accept abortion if a mother's life is at risk or if it will harm her mental health if she continues with the pregnancy. Some rabbis allow abortion where a child is likely to be mentally damaged. They would never allow an abortion for the sake of convenience or for social reasons.

An anti-abortion rally in the USA

INFERTILITY

Raising a family is very important to Jews. The rabbis will allow artificial insemination (when sperm is put into a woman's womb using a surgical instrument) by husband but never by donor. They take strict care to ensure that only the husband's semen is used.

In vitro fertilization (IVF) is when the ovum (egg) is fertilized in a laboratory and then placed in the woman's womb. This can create problems. Some rabbis welcome this procedure, but they insist on very great care being taken.

No one agrees with surrogate motherhood, or 'womb leasing', where another woman has a child on behalf of another. This might lead to women having children without ever being pregnant. It could lead to others making money out of it. Rabbis see this as destroying the sanctity of marriage and childbirth.

Many rabbis think it is wrong to freeze a husband's sperm to use after his death as this 'creates' orphans. However, they would allow it if a man was having treatment that might make him sterile (e.g. for cancer), but was expected to live afterwards.

Jews have always given great spiritual help to childless couples. They say prayers and blessings for them (e.g. *II Kings 4:14–16*). Today, many couples continue seeking medical help after they feel like giving up. This is because of the support of the rabbis.

POINT OF VIEW

Many women believe that they have the right to do what they want with their own body. Judaism does not agree.

FACTFILE

Defining death...

Doctors who transplant human organs need a legal definition of death, to avoid taking organs from a donor before death has occurred. Most countries accept that a person has died when there is 'brain death'. This is the point at which the higher centres of the brain cease to function. It is the moment when it is legal to turn off a life-support system, with permission from the family, and harvest organs for transplantation.

For Jews, the family is very important. This is where husband and wife reach full maturity (see page 76), where children receive their first education (see page 64) and where they form their identity. The **Torah** and the **rabbis** set down basic rules about how families should be run.

HUSBAND AND WIFE

The **ketubah** (marriage document, see page 77) sets out the husband's duty. He promises to support his wife 'even if I have to sell the coat from off my back'. The ketubah also sets out rules for the wife's maintenance in case of a divorce or the husband dying before the wife.

PARENTS AND CHILDREN

'Honour your father and your mother.'

(Exodus 20:12)

Parents and children have responsibilities towards each other. Parents must feed and clothe their children and teach them how to

Illustrated ketubah (nineteenth century)

live as Jews. They must also make sure they train for good jobs. 'Teach your son a trade,' says the **Talmud**, 'or you teach him to be a thief.'

The Talmud also says that parents must teach their children basic survival skills. Today, this would include road safety and being careful about taking lifts from strangers. This may seem like plain good sense, but for Jews it is a religious duty.

Children respect their parents and take care of them. The Talmud says, 'See that they eat and drink, and take them where they need to go.'

If parents make mistakes, children should correct them. However they should do this tactfully so as to avoid hurting their feelings.

THE EXTENDED FAMILY

Lis Harris, a former editor of *New Yorker* magazine, spent some time with a **Hasidic** family (see page 130). The following extract is based on her book about her experiences.

> Bassy, the youngest, who was nineteen, had explained to me that she spent **Shabbat** (Sabbath) with her widowed grandmother who lived around the corner. 'Sometimes she comes here for Shabbat but sometimes she likes to stay at home, so…I stay the night to keep her company.' I said that most girls her age would not be eager to do that. She looked surprised.
>
> 'But I don't mind at all. It's no problem. You'll see when you meet Bubbe (Grandma). She's great. Actually I've

spent every night with her since she had to have a finger removed because of cancer last year.' All the Bubbies and Seydes (grandfathers) felt secure in their families. Personality conflicts happen in Hasidic families as often as anywhere else. But the values of the older and younger members of the family are the same. There is no generation gap.

The importance of the family affects other areas of Jewish life. For example, giving to charity (**tzedakah**, see page 116) comes second to helping one's own close relatives.

FACTFILE

Parents and children

The following story illustrates Jewish teaching about parent–child relationships.

A father once came to Rabbi Israel Baal Shem Tov (1698–1760). 'Rabbi, what shall I do?' the man asked. 'My son is drifting into evil ways.'

'You must love him,' replied the rabbi.

'But Rabbi,' said the father, 'you don't understand. He lies and cheats. He works on the Sabbath. He even steals.'

'In that case,' said Rabbi Israel, 'you must love him even more.'

This story shows that parents who truly love their children can forgive them, and help them to learn better ways.

Sexuality is natural even beyond the age of childbearing

ACCEPTABLE SEXUAL PRACTICE

Jews do not approve of sex outside marriage. However, they believe that sex is an important part of married life. When a husband and wife have sexual intercourse they fulfil the first commandment in the **Torah**, 'Be fruitful and multiply'. Bringing children into the world is seen as a holy act. By starting a family, men and women become partners with God in creating a new life.

Sexuality also helps people to express their love for each other. During a long married life, sexuality is considered to be natural even after the age of childbearing.

FORBIDDEN SEXUAL PRACTICES

For Jews, sexual acts are only acceptable within marriage. The Torah strictly forbids adultery (having sex with someone else's husband or wife). It also forbids incest (sex between close family members, *Leviticus 18:6–23*). Sex between two men is also forbidden (*Leviticus 18:22*). Lesbianism is not mentioned in the Torah, but the **Talmud** disapproves of it.

Homosexual groups have campaigned for greater freedom for their sexual preferences.

They say that homosexuals are different by nature and cannot change. Others strongly believe that homosexuality can develop for various reasons. They say those with homosexual feelings can be 'helped' by regular psychological treatment.

Homosexuality does not include close friendships between people of the same sex. David and Jonathan (King Saul's son, see page 7) had a pure, selfless friendship. It is sexual *activity* between men that Judaism objects to. Men who are attracted to other men are the same as those who are attracted to someone else's wife.

Prostitution is also forbidden in Judaism. Jews see it as degrading and unclean. It makes sex cheap and sordid, and not at all how it should be in a loving, caring married relationship.

Jews also disapprove strongly of the kind of life-style that involves having many sexual partners, of either sex.

Despite their strict views on sexual activity, Jews would not allow men or women who are homosexual to be persecuted. They feel concern for those who are forced into prostitution, or who catch AIDS from sexual contact.

CONTRACEPTION

Jews believe that God created the world '…not to remain empty; He made it to be populated' (*Isaiah 45:18*). He wanted to fill the world with people who would be loyal to Him and make the world holy and a suitable place for God to live (see page 22). Contraception prevents this.

However, Jews believe that life must be protected. If it would be dangerous for a woman to become pregnant, the **rabbis** insist that contraception should be used. This is also true if a pregnancy would cause a woman severe mental strain. It is acceptable to use contraceptives when a woman has just had a baby and could not cope with another straight away. However, Jews do not think it right to use contraception just for the sake of convenience.

Jews believe that it is important that the act of sexual intercourse should be as natural as possible. For this reason the Pill (oral contraception) is the preferred method. Women who cannot take the Pill for medical reasons can use either the diaphragm (Dutch cap) or the intrauterine device (IUD or coil). The IUD can cause heavier and prolonged bleeding during periods, and this would mean husband and wife would not be able to have sexual intercourse until she had visited the **mikveh** (see page 82). This means twelve days without sexual contact.

The condom is not approved of as it is a barrier to complete contact between husband and wife. The femidom presents the same problem.

Vasectomy (cutting the tubes that carry sperm from the testes) is seen as a kind of castration. This is forbidden unless there are medical reasons for doing it. The same applies to sterilization of women.

◇

The Pill, the diaphragm and the IUD are acceptable forms of contraception for Jews

FACTFILE

Acceptable forms of contraception

The Combined Pill is over 99% effective in preventing unwanted pregnancies. It works by stopping the woman's ovaries releasing an egg each month. It is a very safe form of contraception.

The IUD is a small plastic and copper device that a doctor or clinic nurse will fit inside the womb. It is 98–99% effective.

Diaphragms and caps are circular domes made of thin soft rubber with a flexible rim. The diaphragm fits over the cervix. If used correctly they are 92–96% effective.

All these forms are acceptable to most Jews because they allow sex to be as natural as possible.

POINTS OF VIEW

Jews and members of many other religions would not agree with the idea of legalizing prostitution.

'Teach your son a trade, or you teach him to be a thief' (Talmud)

WORK AND THE INDIVIDUAL

'The study of the Torah together with an occupation is an excellent thing.'

(Ethics of the Fathers)

Jews believe that people are put on the earth to serve God (see page 22). They do this through worship and work. A well-balanced person is someone who has a job and who sets time aside to study the **Torah** (see page 65). **Rabbis** in the **Mishnah** say, 'Idleness leads to immorality,' and, 'It leads to depression.' All the rabbis of the **Talmud** had paid jobs. They included a blacksmith, a shoemaker, a farmer, a stonemason, a weaver and a merchant.

Work is something that puts humans above animals. When God sent Adam out of the Garden of Eden (*Genesis 3:17–19*) he told him, 'By the sweat of your face you shall eat bread.' This meant he would be able to earn his own food by working. It is human nature to be able to work, to control the environment and be responsible for it.

Jews believe that by working they are obeying God's will. They believe that people should serve God by being active in the world. They do not think it is right to withdraw and become a monk or a hermit (see page 98).

WORK AND THE COMMUNITY

Work is good both for the individual and for the community. People feel valued when they are productive. A story in the Talmud is about an old man who was planting fruit trees. A Roman officer passing by asked him why he worked so hard for something he would not live to enjoy. The old man replied, 'Just as my father planted for me, so I am planting for my children.'

A community is healthy when every person contributes to the good of society. Unemployment is harmful to individuals and to society. Sometimes unemployment leads to crime. The Talmud says, 'Teach your son a trade, or you teach him to be a thief.' Jews can work at any job they choose. However, they cannot do jobs that may harm people, such as dealing in drugs or pornography. Jews think that these jobs should be forbidden to non-Jews as well!

BUSINESS ETHICS

In business it is sometimes possible to do the right thing for the wrong reasons. For example, a trader with a good reputation for honesty will attract more customers than one with a bad name, so it pays to be honest.

Jewish teaching would say this is not honest at all, because a lot depends on the trader's *intentions*. A business person may give the impression of being honest, while giving bad advice or withholding information. Jewish business ethics are based on fulfilling God's will in intention as well as in actions. When the Torah sets out a rule for business, it usually adds, 'And you shall fear your God'. Jews believe that God knows what a person's intentions really are.

◇

A Jewish summer camp: afternoon prayers in the open air

TRADE RELATIONS

Long before trades unions came into being, **halakhah** (see page 30) set guidelines for industrial relations. In Jewish law everyone is bound by a contract of employment – both employers and workers.

To break the contract is a sin. An employer is bound to pay wages on time. To fail to do so is robbery. An employee must not use working time to do something else. This too is robbery. The rabbis even allowed workers to say some prayers while working, and a short form of grace after meals, so that they would not be robbing their employers.

Employers must not force workers to work longer hours than the contract says. They must follow local customs. For example, if other employers provide a midday meal, then so must the Jewish employers.

LEISURE

For Jews, as for anyone else, leisure can mean many things. Some choose to be entertained, while others prefer to be active or to have hobbies. Some things are not allowed. Jews must not risk their lives unnecessarily. This means no dangerous activities such as hang-gliding or motor racing. Entertainment that goes against Jewish standards of modesty, such as strip-tease, is also forbidden to Jews.

Jews prefer to spend their leisure time in ways that let them keep up the regular observances of Judaism. For example, they may take holidays where they can be sure of praying with a **minyan** (see page 65) and obtaining **kosher** food (see page 68). In Jewish summer camps, there are regular short study sessions (see page 65) so that they can keep up daily study of the Torah.

FACTFILE

Give God glory

G M Hopkins was a Christian writer, but what he said about work reflects the Jewish work ethic.

'It is not only prayer that gives God glory but work. Smiting on an anvil, sawing a beam, whitewashing a wall, driving horses, sweeping, scouring, everything gives God some glory…To lift up the hands in prayer gives God glory, but a man with a dung fork in his hand, a woman with a slop pail, give him glory too. He is so great that all things give him glory if you mean they should.'

People did not always think that 'ordinary people' had much value. Those who kept slaves did not even think of them as people. Aristotle, a Greek thinker who lived over 2000 years ago, wrote, 'A slave is a human tool just as a tool is an inanimate [i.e. non-living] slave'. The serfs of the Middle Ages were little better than slaves. In Britain only a century ago, the upper classes were known as 'the quality'. Ordinary people had little worth.

The idea that every human being has worth, and therefore human rights, comes from the teachings of the **Torah** and the prophets. It reached western countries as Christianity spread and taught these ideas.

RIGHTS AND RESPONSIBILITIES

Judaism teaches that every human being is created for a purpose and is part of God's plan (see page 22). People must have basic rights and freedoms, to fulfil this purpose. However, people who have rights also have responsibilities. *Genesis* 6:5 says that at one time people had been so wicked that there was 'only evil the whole day'. No one in the whole world was doing a single good deed. They were not doing what God had put them in the world to do. As a result they lost the most basic human right - the right to live. God destroyed them with a flood.

Today, while we hear a lot about people's rights, we hear less about responsibilities. For example, trade unions speak of the workers' right to strike. They say little about the small traders who may be ruined if their workers go on strike. Jewish teaching is that rights and responsibilities go together. A person has the right to lead his or her own life in the way they want. However, it is wrong for people to express their rights at the expense of others, for example to hold noisy parties or do other things to upset their neighbours.

THE SOURCE OF HUMAN RIGHTS

Some of the most basic human rights can be found in the **Noachide Laws** which Jews feel apply to all human beings (see page 20).

The right to life: The Laws forbid murder. By commanding people not to take life, it states that human beings have the right to live.

Jews believe life is sacred (holy) because God gave it (*Genesis 2:7*). Normally only God may take it (*Deuteronomy 32:39*). Jews believe that human life is necessary because every human being is part of God's plan. For this reason Judaism does not agree with suicide and euthanasia (see page 103). A foetus (unborn baby) has the right to live, as every child born is also a person with a part to play in God's plan (see page 106). Judaism usually allows abortion only if there is a risk to the mother's life.

The right to own property, and to freedom of movement: The Laws also forbid theft. In Jewish teaching, theft includes kidnapping and taking hostages. This means that all individuals and organizations have the right to own possessions. People have the right to go about their daily lives freely.

The right not to be abused sexually: No one has the right to force someone else into a sexual relationship. The Laws forbid adultery, as everyone has the right to the unique love and care of their spouses (partners in marriage).

The right to a just legal system: Judaism recognizes that governments have both the right and the duty to make laws for the benefit of their people, and to enforce them. 'The law of the land is the law' says the **Talmud**.

However, Jews do not regard laws that take away people's human rights to be binding.

The United Nations General Assembly

THE UNIVERSAL DECLARATION OF HUMAN RIGHTS

The Universal Declaration of Human Rights was drawn up in 1948. In 1976 this became law in the 45 countries (including Britain) that accepted them. Some of the terms of the Declaration are:

- No one shall be arrested, detained or exiled (expelled from their country) without good cause.

- Everyone charged with a punishable offence must be presumed innocent until proven guilty.

- Everyone has the right to freedom of movement. They can leave any country.

- Everyone has the right to work, to a free choice of employment, to just and fair conditions of employment and to protection against unemployment.

- Everyone has the right to a standard of living sufficient for health and well-being. Mothers and children are entitled to special care.

Jews strongly approve of the Declaration. The rules reflect the teachings of the **Tenakh** and other Jewish teachings about morality.

FACTFILE

Prejudice and discrimination

Prejudice is *thinking* about people unfavourably without good reason. Discrimination is *acting* unfairly towards groups of people. The Bible forbids this:

'And if a stranger should live in your country, you must do him no wrong. The stranger who lives with you shall be as the home-born among you, and you shall love him like yourself'

(Leviticus 19:33–34)

Racism is discrimination against a person's race or skin colour.

Ethnic discrimination is against different religious or cultural groups.

Snobbery may cause discrimination against a social class.

QUOTE

Every human being has been given free-will. If he wishes…to be righteous …or to be wicked, he is free to do so.

(Mishnah)

'Who is rich? He who is satisfied with what he has.'

(Ethics of the Fathers)

Jews believe that each **Rosh Hashanah** (New Year, see page 44), God decides how rich a person will be. However, Jews also believe that people have to work to provide the means by which God will bless them.

WEALTH

Judaism discourages materialism, the desire for money and possessions. At the same time it recognizes that people need to have some possessions if they are to serve God properly. There has to be a middle way between desiring wealth and rejecting it.

'…let me be neither rich nor poor…If I have more, I might say I do not need You. But if I am poor I might steal and bring disgrace on my God.'

(Proverbs 30:8–9)

The **Torah** warns people that materialism can take people away from God.

'When you have all you want to eat and have built good houses to live in and when your cattle and sheep, your silver and gold,…have increased,… do not become proud and forget the Lord your God…'

(Deuteronomy 8:12–14)

Wealth is only good for what it can buy. The **Mishnah** says that when a person dies, the only things he takes with him are '…the Torah he has learnt and the good works he has carried out.'

POVERTY

Although Judaism discourages materialism, it does not turn poverty into something to be admired. 'Poverty is worse than fifty plagues,' says the **Talmud**. Jews are expected to give a tenth of their income to helping those worse off than themselves. They are taught that they should not think of that tenth as their own. However, they should decide which charity to give it to. They believe that to keep all one's wealth is to steal from the poor.

Jews expect even the very poor to give something, though not the whole tenth. They believe that everyone has a responsibility to help people in need – even those who are themselves in need.

CHARITY

For the Jew there are two kinds of charity: giving of one's *wealth* (money) and giving of *oneself*.

Giving money is called **tzedakah** (righteousness).

It is tzedakah to give money directly to a poor person. However, this might cause feelings of embarrassment. It is better to give in such a way that the giver does not know who receives, and the receiver does not know who has given (see page 59).

One way to avoid embarrassment is to think of the donation as a loan. The receiver does not need to feel awkward. The giver does not expect the loan to be repaid, but the receiver can feel he or she will repay 'some day'.

The problem with tzedakah is that often the poor remain poor and soon need more help. The best thing is to help a poor person to become self supporting. This preserves the poor person's sense of dignity or pride.

Jews apply similar rules to giving to famine-stricken countries. They look beyond the emergency. They are happier to help in relief programmes that provide farmers with equipment and teach them to use fertilizers to help themselves.

Giving of oneself, that is one's own time and effort, is called **gemilut hassadim** (good deeds). This may involve looking after sick or old people, taking care of children when families are in difficulties and giving comfort to mourners. The rich can give tzedakah – but everyone in the community can become involved in gamilut hassadim.

Many Jewish homes keep collection boxes for worthy causes, called **pushkes**. Family members, including the children, regularly put money in the pushke.

◇

REFLECTION

'I was in hospital having Esther when my husband was rushed in with appendicitis. My neighbours were fantastic. All my children were found places to stay and there was a rota of helpers for when I came home. By the time my sister arrived, there was really nothing for her to do.'

(Mrs W, North London)

◇

No home to go to: poverty in a city of plenty

FACTFILE

Materialism

Materialism can have two meanings. It means having a great interest in and the desire to possess money and goods. It can also mean the rejection of any spiritual or religious ideas.

◇

FACTFILE

Degrees of charity

Maimonides (see page 32) created a list of eight 'degrees' of charity in descending order of their worth:

1 To help people to help themselves by giving a loan or finding them jobs

2 To give anonymously

3 To give in a way that the donor knows who receives, but the recipient does not know the donor

4 The opposite of (3)

5 To give before being asked

6 To give only when asked

7 To give cheerfully – but less than one should

8 To give grudgingly

Since the earliest days, Jews have always thought it was important to care for the disadvantaged, those with needs. The Psalms describe how God cares for them:

'The Lord gives food to the hungry, the Lord frees those imprisoned, the Lord opens the eyes of the blind, the Lord raises up those who are bowed down, the Lord takes care of strangers, He supports orphans and widows.'

(Psalm 146:7–9)

The **Talmud** encourages people to follow God's example:

'Just as God visits the sick, feeds the hungry and clothes the naked, so you do the same.'

SPECIAL NEEDS

The **rabbis** always made allowances for people with disabilities. For example, on **Shabbat** Jews are forbidden to carry anything out into the street. However, people who need help with walking could take a walking stick or crutches.

Jews are forbidden to operate machinery on Shabbat. However, life-saving equipment, such as pacemakers for hearts, is allowed. This is because preserving a life takes first place.

CARE ORGANIZATIONS

Judaism teaches that disadvantage is everyone's problem. It is not just up to the poor and people with disabilities to solve their own problems.

Jews regard helping the disadvantaged as a task for the whole community. Since ancient times, Jews have set up care organizations for those in need. In the past these mainly distributed food and money to the poor and those in need. They taxed Jewish communities to help to provide these things. The elderly always had special treatment. The teaching 'Honour your father and your mother' (*Exodus 20:12*) means people should respect any elderly person. Those

A Jewish teenager helps at a retirement home

whose minds may be failing must be treated with dignity.

JEWISH CARE AGENCIES IN BRITAIN

Norwood Child Care

This began in 1795 as a Jewish orphanage with 20 children. Today it acts as a social service agency for Jewish children. Norwood helps families with problems, especially if there is a child with a disability. It also helps people to cope with unemployment and drug and alcohol problems. Some families may need extra money for clothes for their children, or for a holiday they could not afford. Norwood's trained staff give foster care and counselling to young people suffering from violence or neglect, drug dependency or anorexia.

Jewish Care

The Jewish Welfare Board, the Jewish Blind Society and the Jewish Association for the Disabled combined to form Jewish Care. It provides sheltered housing for the disabled. This lets them be independent, while help is close at hand. Jewish Care also runs residential homes for people with mental health problems, and day centres for the elderly. It sends trained care staff to help house-bound people with dressing, washing and meals.

Chai-Lifeline

This Jewish agency supports cancer patients and their families during this difficult time. It offers counselling and alternative treatments.

Another organization supported by donations from British Jews is Magen David Adom, the Israel Ambulance Service.

CARING FOR THE CARERS

Not many Jewish care organizations receive local council grants. Most have to raise money from voluntary donations. Jews raise the money in many ways – through sponsored walks and appeals in Jewish newspapers. Many Jews have collection boxes in their homes (see page 117). Some leave money to care organizations in their wills. All these are expressions of **tzedakah** (see page 116). Volunteering to work alongside trained staff is a way of expressing **gemilut hassadim** (see page 117).

Jews do not only support their own care organizations. They contribute to any deserving cause that needs aid.

FACTFILE

Project Renewal

Project Renewal started in the late 1970s. It is a joint effort between the Israeli Government and Jewish groups outside Israel. It aims to rebuild poor areas and improve facilities for the residents. National and local government officers and committees of residents work together to find solutions to longstanding problems such as housing, employment, education, health and community services. Today over 80 Jewish communities outside Israel are 'twinned' with particular areas. They give financial and practical help.

KEY WORD

Disadvantaged people – people who suffer from disability or handicap, which may be physical or social.

THE ROLE OF GOVERNMENT

Here is a story from the **Talmud** about the difference between good and bad government.

King Alexander the Great once visited King Katzia. He said he wanted to see how justice was carried out in this country. Just then, two men came to King Katzia. The first said, 'Your majesty, this man sold me a field. When I dug it, I found a treasure. I want him to take the treasure back because I only paid him for the field.'

The other replied, 'No. I sold him the field and so anything he finds in it belongs to him.' King Katzia said to the first man, 'Do you have a son?' 'Yes,' he replied. Katzia asked the other man, 'Do you have a daughter?' 'Yes.' 'Then let your son marry his daughter and give them the treasure as a wedding present,' ruled King Katzia.

King Alexander began to laugh. Katzia asked him, 'What would you have done?' 'I would have killed them both and kept the treasure for myself,' replied Alexander. Katzia was shocked. 'Does it rain in your country?' he asked. 'Yes,' replied Alexander. 'Are there cattle in your country?' 'Yes.' 'Well,' said Katzia, 'if that is justice in your country, then only the cattle deserve the rain. The people do not deserve it.'

THINKING POINT

What do you think the above story says about good and bad government?

THE LAW OF THE LAND

In Biblical times almost all Jews lived in the country now known as Israel. The law of the land was the **Torah** and Jews obeyed it because they believed it to be God's will (see page 104). By the end of the first century CE Jews were scattered throughout the world. They had to live by the laws of the Torah and the laws of the country in which they lived. If the law of the land was different from the Torah, the **rabbis** ruled that 'the law of the land is the law'.

This did not apply to the commandments of the Torah. For example, in the second century BCE a Greek-Syrian king tried to force the Jews to change their religion (see page 56). The Jews disobeyed him and rose up against him to fight for their right to worship as they wished.

JUSTICE

'You shall appoint judges and officers in all your towns …and they shall judge the people righteously.'

(Deuteronomy 16:18)

From the earliest times the Jewish legal system consisted of three levels of **bet din** or court. Ordinary trials were conducted by a court of three judges. They questioned the witnesses and reached a verdict. For an offence that called for the death penalty, a bet din of 23 judges was needed. Matters of national importance called for a **Sanhedrin**, a court of 71 judges (see page 97).

Discussing a case in the London Bet Din

THE DEATH PENALTY

In Jewish law the death penalty was imposed for serious offences such as murder, raping a married woman or breaking the Sabbath. This was intended as a punishment, but also allowed the offender to atone (make amends) for his or her offence.

A person could only be executed if witnesses had first given a warning of the punishment, and had then actually seen the crime carried out in front of them. If people heard a scream, then rushed into a room and saw a man standing over a body holding a knife dripping with blood there would be no death penalty. No one had actually witnessed the crime.

The death penalty was rarely carried out. It was there to show which crimes were the most serious. The **Mishnah** says that a bet din that executed a person once in 70 years was a 'destructive bet din'. No Jewish court has carried out a death sentence since Roman times.

'AN EYE FOR AN EYE'

This misunderstood verse (*Exodus 21:24*) actually means compensation in money. It is designed to limit the amount of punishment to be handed out for injuring someone. It must be *no more than* the value of an eye for an eye.

BET DIN TODAY

Today there is only the bet din of three judges. They are very experienced and learned rabbis. There are several rabbinic courts, mainly to deal with divorce cases, conversions and business disputes between Jews. Bet din have strict rules about who may take part. Witnesses must not have a criminal record or be known as dishonest. Judges must be strictly impartial and not known personally to the parties in dispute.

FACTFILE 1

Israel's court system

There are four main courts in Israel:

Magistrates' Courts, with one judge, deal with minor criminal cases.

The District Court may have one or three judges. These deal with more important cases, and Magistrates Courts can refer cases up to this court.

The Supreme Court has one, three or five judges. The is the court of 'ultimate appeal'. It has power to over-rule other courts if they go too far, or to hear cases against important persons and politicians, or the most important criminal cases.

The Religious Courts include rabbinical courts for Jews. They hear cases relating to marriage and divorce. There are also special religious courts for Muslims and **Druse**, and for Christians.

FACTFILE 2

Fair punishment

Punishments in the Torah were *proportional* to the offences – 'an eye for an eye, a tooth for a tooth'.

'The world stands on three things, on justice, on truth and on peace.'

(Ethics of the Fathers)

PEACE AS AN IDEAL

When Jews meet, or are parting, they say, '**Shalom**!' – peace. Jews have always hated war and they hope that one day the world will live in peace. Judaism does not teach total pacifism (the avoidance of war). There are times when a nation has to fight. But it does teach that they must do their best to avoid war (e.g. *II Kings 6:21–23*).

OBLIGATORY AND OPTIONAL WARS

For Jews, wars are either obligatory (they *must* be fought) or optional (they are the only way to resolve a particular problem).

Obligatory wars

After Moses died, God commanded Joshua to lead the Israelites into the Promised Land. It was occupied by other tribes and the Israelites would have to fight for it. That war was an obligatory war – one that God commanded the Israelites to fight.

Jews feel it is a religious duty to defend their lives and the lives of their families. A war that is fought in self-defence is an obligatory war.

The third kind of obligatory war is the pre-emptive war – striking an enemy who is about to attack. In 1967 Israel learned that Egypt and Syria were about to attack their country. The Israeli Air Force attacked the airfields of those countries and destroyed most of their aircraft. The war was over in six days. The lives of many Jews and Arabs were spared.

It is also an obligatory war to go to the aid of a country that is under attack to prevent the war reaching one's own country. In 1939, the British Government declared war on Germany when it had begun to invade Poland and other European countries. They realized that if the German armies were not stopped, they would invade Britain. Jews would regard this as an obligatory war.

Optional wars

An optional war can only be fought if there are good reasons for fighting and diplomacy has failed. The **Sanhedrin** (see page 97) has to approve it (though there has not been a Sanhedrin since Roman times). For example, in the tenth century BCE, hostile neighbours had been attacking and plundering Israeli border towns for three centuries. King David decided the only way to end this was to declare war on them. The court gave their approval and David won a lasting peace.

A NON-MILITARY HERITAGE

Jews do not glorify war. They do not have heroes such as the knights of Europe, or the Japanese samurai. The earliest Israelite army was formed in order to take the Holy Land (see page 7). Later, the tribes were called up to fight whenever they had to defend their land. As soon as the battles were over the men went back to their farms.

The **Talmud** teaches that warfare comes to the world whenever justice is delayed or when there is injustice.

MARTYRDOM

Although Jews place great value on life, they believe that sometimes they must give up their lives for their beliefs. Martyrdom is called **kiddush hashem**, sanctifying the

An Israeli soldier prepared for war but praying for peace

Name of God. Jews may be expected to give up their lives rather than commit one of the three most serious sins. These are: murder, idolatry or sexual immorality.

During the **Holocaust** six million Jews were killed simply because they were Jews. These people are known as **kedoshim**, holy ones. Many faced death bravely and inspired others to die praising God. Not everyone shared the same attitude to martyrdom. The Nazis shot **Rabbi** Elchonon Wasserman in 1941. As he faced the firing squad he told his fellow-Jews:

'…if we repent we will become better sacrifices…no wrong thought must enter anyone's mind…we are now going to perform the greatest **mitzvah**…'

However, just before the Warsaw Ghetto uprising in 1943, Rabbi Menachem Zemba said:

'There is absolutely no purpose nor any value in kiddush hashem, in the death of a Jew. Kiddush hashem in our present situation means the will of a Jew to live. This struggle for life is a mitzvah.'

PEACE

Peace is not just the absence of war. It means having such friendship between nations that war becomes unthinkable. Jews believe that universal peace will finally come in the time of the Messiah (see page 24). Then 'They will beat their swords into plough shares and their spears into pruning hooks. Nation shall not lift up sword against nation nor shall they train for war any more' (*Isaiah 2:4*). Jews praise each move towards peace as a step nearer to a time of universal, lasting peace.

FACTFILE 1

Israel Defence Forces (IDF)
The IDF was founded at the same time as the State of Israel in 1948. Israel believes its Forces are the most battle-trained armed forces in the world, having been involved in five major wars in less than 45 years.

FACTFILE 2

The Peace Process
After many years of war, Israel tried to make peace with its Arab neighbours, and with Palestinians. In 1991 there was a peace conference in Madrid to which Israel, Syria, Jordan and the Palestinians sent representatives. In 1993 Israel and the PLO (Palestine Liberation Organization) agreed to recognize each other's rights within Palestine and the PLO pledged itself to 'a peaceful resolution of the conflict'. In 1994 Israel and Jordan signed a peace treaty in the presence of US President Clinton.

POINT OF VIEW

Many parents who are opposed to war do not allow their children to play with toy guns.

ANIMALS IN THE TORAH

Kindness to animals is important to Jews. The **Noachide Laws** (see page 20) forbid cruelty to animals.

The **Torah** describes the creation of animals:

> '...God made the animals according to their kinds, the beasts according to their kinds and all the things that creep upon the earth.'

It then says that God gave humans 'control over the fish of the sea and the birds of the sky, over the animals and over the whole earth' (*Genesis 1:20–26*).

Jews interpret these verses to mean that:

- animals are God's creatures and must be respected because of that
- animal life does not have the same value as human life.

Animals work for people and give us certain raw materials. They have a place in the balance of nature that helps to make the planet a fit place for humans to live.

The Torah teaches that beasts of burden should rest on **Shabbat** (*Deuteronomy 5:14*). At harvest time, the horse or ox pulling a wagon should not be muzzled, so that it could eat crops as it worked (*Deuteronomy 25:4*). A farmer should not allow an ox and donkey to pull a plough together as it would put too much strain on the donkey (*Deuteronomy 22:11*). There are many similar teachings about animal welfare.

THE TALMUD

The **Talmud** teaches that a farmer should feed his animals before sitting down to his own meal. He should not buy more animals than he could afford to keep. The **rabbis** even relaxed the Sabbath laws to allow a farmer to help an animal that had fallen into a pit.

Rules like these mean that Jews feel strongly about animal rights. They are disgusted by cruelty to animals.

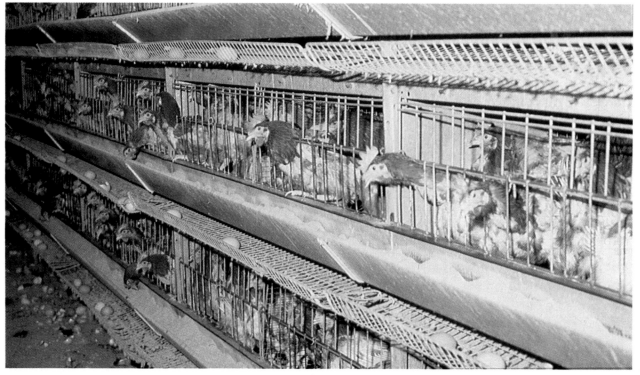

Battery hens: Jews would not approve of this way of treating animals

ANIMALS FOR FOOD

There is no rule anywhere that says Jews must eat meat. They may become vegetarian if they wish. However, if people choose to eat meat, Judaism insists that they must kill the animals in as pain-free a way as possible. For Jews this means **shechitah** – the most painless method known for killing animals. This is described in Unit 33.

EXPERIMENTS ON ANIMALS

Judaism has to consider two things when looking at the issue of experiments on animals. First, the Noachide Laws and Jewish law forbid inflicting unnecessary pain on animals. Second, Jews do not regard animal life as having the same value as human life. They believe that animals can be used to further human needs.

This rules out experiments on animals for cosmetics. Humans do not *need* cosmetics.

Medical experiments are different. Jews believe that finding cures for diseases, or practising surgical operations, are very important human needs. Many killer diseases such as diphtheria, smallpox and polio have been almost wiped out because of the success of experiments with animals. Surgeons have learned to transplant hearts, kidneys and livers by operating on animals before working on people.

Jews will allow experiments on animals only if there is no other way to fight disease. All experiments must be carefully controlled to cause as little pain as possible. Judaism forbids cruel sports such as bullfighting.

FACTFILE

More teachings about animals

The Talmud tells the story of **Rabbi** Judah who once saw a calf being led to the slaughter-house. The calf ran towards him and hid its head in his robe as if to ask for his protection. The rabbi said, 'Go, this is what you were created for.' That day it was decided in heaven that, as he had shown the calf no kindness, he should be made to suffer. A few weeks later, his servant was cleaning the house and wanted to turn out some young weasels that had made a nest there. Rabbi Judah called out, 'Leave them. God's mercy includes all his creatures.' On that day it was decided that his sufferings should end.

'Teachers must see that children respect the smallest and largest animals which, like people, have feelings. The child who gets enjoyment from the [suffering] of an injured beetle will grow up to be insensitive to human suffering.'
(Rabbi Samson Raphael Hirsch, 1808–1888)

QUOTE

If you chance to come upon a bird's nest and the mother sitting…you shall let the mother go.

(Deuteronomy 22:6–7)

'The earth and everything that fills it is the Lord's…'

(Psalm 24:1)

GOD'S PLANET

The book of *Genesis* in the **Torah** describes the stages in which God created the earth for humans to live on. He made a climate, separated the land from the seas, created plant life and animal life. Finally, He created the first human couple (see page 20).

The Torah says that human beings were to till the ground and look after it (*Genesis 2:15*). Jews believe that God wants people to serve Him and make this world a place where He can one day come to live (see page 22). That is, this is God's planet, not ours. People have the responsibility to use the world's resources wisely.

DO NOT DESTROY

The Torah says clearly that humans should not destroy anything without a good reason. In ancient times an army attacking a city would lay siege (surround it) so that no one could go in or leave. Jews were commanded not to cut down fruit trees for their siege walls:

'When you lay siege to a city…you must not destroy its trees by taking up an axe against them;…for the tree of the field is man's life…'

(Deuteronomy 20:19)

In the oral Torah (see page 25) this is understood to mean that no one should ever waste things.

CONSERVATION

Jews may have been the first to set up a green belt around towns. They believe that conservation should benefit people. From the earliest days a green area, called a **migrash** (*Numbers 35:2*), was set up around towns.

Unlike many green belts of today, the migrash was to be kept as open land (not used for golf courses, cemeteries or rubbish tips). No one could set up a business or grow crops there. It was purely for the enjoyment of the people. It helped to limit the size of towns, too.

In ancient times all cities in Israel had a migrash and sometimes a ring of fruit trees. Today in Israel, the Jewish National Fund helps to finance the planting of trees. Its slogan is 'Working for a greener Israel'.

Cutting down rain forests in Brazil: is this development or destruction?

POLLUTION

Everyone can help to control pollution by not dropping litter, by recycling and by not wasting energy. Judaism teaches that this helps to maintain people's health and well-being. These are more important than profits. For example, the **Talmud** says that businesses that cause pollution must be kept away from towns and always away from the prevailing winds.

Modern industry produces a great deal of waste. Much of this is toxic (poisonous). It can take the form of smoke, liquid or solid wastes. If poured into the sea or buried in landfills, it can poison fish, the soil, plants and animals. It enters the human food chain. Judaism believes it is essential for *all* industry to be able to deal with *all* its waste *before* they start working.

THE MORAL DIMENSION

A zoologist (animal scientist) in Africa once allowed himself to be killed by a white rhino rather than shoot it because it was a member of an endangered species. A British motorist swerved to avoid a swan – and killed another driver.

This shows a new way of thinking that Jews think is misguided and dangerous. It leads to the view that people are no more important than animals or insects.

For Jews, whenever the environment and the needs of human beings come into conflict, a *moral* decision has to be made. People have to decide what ought to be done. Jews believe that humans have the greatest value, and a special place in creation.

For example, should rainforests be cut down to make room for farms? For Jews it is not just a question of whether there will be enough trees left to deal with the carbon dioxide. It is a human question. If the trees are cut down, then tribes who live in the forest lose their homes and their way of life. If they are not, there will be not enough land for the poor farmers to make a living. There are no easy answers.

◇

KEY WORD

Conservation – keeping the environment from harm, or protecting it

FACTFILE

The Jewish National Fund

The JNF was set up in 1901 to buy land in Palestine (the earlier name for Israel) for Jewish people. Up to 1948, when the State of Israel was founded, it had bought 96 000 hectares. Most of this land had been neglected and allowed to become almost like a desert. The JNF began by planting about 4 million trees to help to restore the land and make it fit for farming. Today the JNF is concerned with helping to develop new settlements. It continues its work of maintaining forests, greening hillsides and preparing trails and picnic areas.

There are now about 200 million trees in Israel and it is once again a land of green hillsides, a land 'flowing with milk and honey'.

WHAT IS ORTHODOXY?

Jews have always believed that their religion involves a covenant (two-way promise) with God (see page 22). They believe that their part of the covenant is to observe the **mitzvot** (God's commandments). Orthodox Jews are those who accept that traditional Jewish beliefs and practices are important. This can apply to Jews who are fully observant, as well as those who do not attend worship regularly. This unit and Units 64 and 65 are about styles of Judaism that follow orthodox thinking.

THE RISE OF LITHUANIA

During the early seventeenth century, Poland had the largest population of Jews in Europe. The most famous **yeshivot** (Talmudic academies) were also in Poland.

In 1648 Cossack troops poured into Poland from the Ukraine. They killed thousands of Poles and Jews. They were beaten back, but then Russia invaded Poland and many more Jews were killed. Then, the Poles suspected the Jews of working for the Russians. As the Russians left, the Poles wiped out many Jewish communities. The next year, there was an epidemic (disease) that killed many more. This was a disaster for Jews in Poland. By the end of the century Poland was no longer a centre of Jewish life and learning. Lithuania began to emerge as the new centre for **Torah** learning in Europe.

RABBI ELIJAH OF VILNA (1720–1797)

Rabbi Elijah of Vilna was known as the Vilna Gaon (the genius of Vilna). He was the father of Lithuanian orthodoxy. He set out to rebuild Jewish life firmly based on study of the Torah. His students became teachers and rabbis. They spread Torah learning through Lithuania and other parts of Europe.

Rabbi Elijah was a **lamdan**, a man with great knowledge and understanding of the **Talmud** and other Jewish literature. He was a role model for his students. He devoted himself day and night to his studies of the Torah, Talmud, codes and commentaries (see page 31).

In 1803, Rabbi Elijah's best student, Rabbi Chaim, established a yeshiva in Volozhin. This academy only accepted the best students and it set very high standards. Its teaching methods were copied by other yeshivot, and by other Jewish study groups at synagogues throughout Lithuania. Young men trained in Lithuania went all over the world as rabbis and teachers. Wherever they went, they established yeshivot and study groups. They aimed to spread Lithuanian-style orthodoxy.

THE MUSAR MOVEMENT

The **Musar movement** aimed to improve the character training of Jews.

During the late eighteenth century the **maskilim** (followers of **Haskalah**, see page 10) wanted the Jews to change their language, dress and manners and have ordinary subjects taught in Jewish schools. The **Hasidim** (see Unit 64) opposed this and Haskalah was unsuccessful in Poland. However, it had some success in Lithuania.

By the mid-nineteenth century two Jewish political movements emerged in Russia: the Bund, (see page 11) and Zionism (see page 144). The Bund was a Jewish socialist group. The Zionists wanted to create a Jewish homeland in Palestine.

These movements had new ideas about Judaism. Some of these ideas reached the yeshivot. Students read political pamphlets in their rooms or hid them inside copies of the Talmud. Many neglected their Jewish observance.

RABBI ISRAEL LIPKIN OF SALANT (1810–1883)

In about 1842, Rabbi Israel Lipkin set up a **chevrat musar** (society for studying religious ethics) in Vilna. They republished several medieval books about ethics (see page 33) and wanted people to study them. Rabbi Israel also set up a study room where people could spend time reflecting on their character.

Businessmen were not interested in chevrat musar, but Rabbi Israel's efforts encouraged many yeshivot in Lithuania to study musar.

WHAT MUSAR IS ABOUT

Musar aims to help people to improve their character and become better in serving God. Musar writings show how pride, envy, greed and sloth (laziness) prevent people from serving God as they should. They stressed the importance of humility, love, compassion and devotion and showed how to develop these. There were lectures about character improvement. Teachers taught students to look within themselves and to apply the lessons of the musar books.

By the 1880s there were many yeshiva graduates who were devoted to traditional Judaism. They expected high standards of morality and religious observance in their business and working lives.

Today most yeshivot and girls' seminaries teach musar, though methods vary from place to place. In synagogues, rabbis encourage their people to develop their characters and remain true to their faith.

FACTFILE

A righteous person

Judaism has always been concerned with ethics – the basis upon which people decide what is right or wrong.

An ancient tradition says that the world continues to exist because of the righteousness of thirty-six people. A person so good is a truly saintly soul.

Hebrew letters also stand for numbers. The letters that add up to number '36' are *lamed* and *vav*. A saintly person is called a *lamedvavnik*.

Yeshiva students study in pairs (the chavruta system)

'If a person is attached to God then he is truly alive.'

(Rabbi Israel Baal Shem Tov)

After the disasters of the seventeenth century (see Unit 63), the Jews who survived in Poland were mainly poor people who had to work long hours to make a living. They did not have much opportunity for study. By 1730 three generations had grown up with hardly any Jewish education.

Jews were depressed. They recited psalms and prayed with devotion, but without **Torah** study they felt they were imperfect as Jews. The Torah scholars of Lithuania (see Unit 63) tended to look down on them.

RABBI ISRAEL BAAL SHEM TOV (1698–1760)

Rabbi Israel Baal Shem Tov (which means 'Master of the Good Name', i.e. the Name of God) was a member of a group of 'hidden mystics'. He travelled round Jewish communities to encourage uneducated village people to improve their Jewish observance. He soon gained many followers among the village people.

Rabbi Israel taught the **kabbalah** (see page 33) in a simple form for ordinary people.

He said that people should become 'attached' to God. They needed only to pray sincerely and carry out the **mitzvot** with enthusiasm. He said that God loves the simple Jew who can read the psalms with sincerity as much as He loves the most learned scholar. He told the poor that they had an advantage over the scholars, who often suffered from feelings of pride. Above all he stressed the importance of serving God with joy. Ordinary people found such teachings a breath of fresh air. They began to feel that God really did love them. They were ready to pray and carry out mitzvot with enthusiasm and joy.

THE HASIDIM

Rabbi Israel is best known for his work with ordinary people. However, the scholars he taught also liked his approach. He said that kabbalah could shine through their Judaism. His way of serving God with joy, and the love he showed to ordinary people, attracted them. His followers became known as **Hasidim** (pious ones).

Other scholars opposed the Hasidim. They were worried that Rabbi Israel might be a false messiah (see page 24). They felt some Hasidim seemed more involved with joyous service than with Talmudic study.

Habad Hasidim conducting a children's rally on Lag b'Omer (see page 62)

THE MOVEMENT EXPANDS

When Rabbi Israel died, his leading student, Rabbi Dov Baer of Mezrich, became leader of the Hasidim. He encouraged a few close disciples (students) to become future leaders. By the time Rabbi Dov Baer died in 1772, there were centres in Poland, Galicia, Russia and the Ukraine.

The towns where the disciples settled became the new centres of the **Hasidic movement**. People turned to the **rebbe** (Hasidic leader) for guidance on Jewish matters, but also on general issues, such as problems with children or starting a business. The first Hasidic group outside Europe was started in 1778 in the Holy Land.

The **rebbeim** (plural of rebbe) continued to educate ordinary people. By the mid-1930s there were several million Hasidim in eastern Europe.

HASIDIM TODAY

During the **Holocaust** (see page 16) the Hasidim suffered terrible losses. Many towns were wiped out. Hasidim who survived fled to the west and to Israel (then Palestine).

Today there are Hasidic groups in London, Jerusalem, New York, Antwerp, Melbourne, Rio de Janeiro and many other cities. They live in close-knit communities. They have their own schools, synagogues and **yeshivot**. Many still wear the traditional dress of a long black coat and large black hat. On **Shabbat** and festivals, they wear knee-length breeches and fur hats. They speak a dialect of **Yiddish**. Hasidic women dress very modestly.

Hasidim are strict in observing the mizvot and serve God with great joy. Their synagogue services are lively, happy events. They tend to marry within the Hasidic movement. Divorce rates are very low. Families stay close together and share each other's joys and sorrows.

Habad Hasidim (also known as Lubavitch, after a town in Russia) are different. While other Hasidim have little contact with the world, Habad Hasidim are concerned with everyone, Jews and non-Jews. They may wear Western clothes and speak the language of the country where they live. They run the largest Jewish educational network in the world.

FACTFILE

Clothing

There are various rules about what Jews may and may not wear. A mitzvah says that Jews must not wear the clothing of members of the opposite sex. This is taken to refer to men who wear women's clothes for immoral purposes.

During times of religious persecution, Jews were forced to wear distinctive 'Jewish' clothes. This actually became a means of preventing the majority population from swamping the Jewish character.

Hasidim today still wear clothes that reflect this period. Their fur-trimmed hat (shtreiml) and long black caftan were the dress of Polish noblemen of the eighteenth century.

Poles, Russians and Ukrainians thought of the Jews who lived in eastern Europe as foreigners. However, in western Europe the **Haskalah** (see page 10) encouraged Jews to become more like their neighbours. Many Jews living in Germany were hardly different from non-Jews. Some even became Christians.

The Reform movement (see Unit 67) began at about this time. Its leaders said that Judaism had to change to fit in with modern society. They cut the prayers short and had organs in synagogues. Some did away with circumcision, and held **Shabbat** on Sunday.

Traditional **rabbis** thought that reform would result in Judaism losing out as a religion and tried to oppose it. They did not succeed, and the Reform movement spread rapidly. However, many Jews wanted to keep traditional Judaism and to make it fit in with modern European life. Neo-Orthodoxy came about to fill this need.

RABBI SAMSON RAPHAEL HIRSCH (1808–1888)

During the early nineteenth century, some rabbis in Germany tried to find ways to let Judaism and the rest of society to work together. Rabbi Samson Raphael Hirsch found such a way. It became known as neo (or new) Orthodoxy. He saw the problems for Jews wanting to living in a free society. He did not accept that the religion had to be reformed. He wrote, 'It is Jews who need reforming, not Judaism.' He pointed out that Judaism has the highest ideals of religion and morality. Jews must live by their beliefs. They must not change Judaism to make it fit society, as the reformers were doing.

In 1836 Rabbi Hirsch published *Nineteen Letters on Judaism*. These were written as an exchange of letters between a young German-Jewish scholar and a traditional Jew.

The *Nineteen Letters* explain that Judaism can work perfectly well with modern culture.

Rabbi Samson Raphael Hirsch

Judaism can help a person to have the best possible character. Young German Jews were very impressed with the book and many wanted Rabbi Hirsch to become their leader.

In 1851 Hirsch became rabbi of an Orthodox synagogue in Frankfurt. He set up three schools, including a high school for girls. There, students learned Hebrew and Jewish subjects, as well as German, mathematics and science. In the synagogue, Hirsch preached in German, and introduced a choir and singing for the congregation.

Hirsch felt the ideal person was the *Israel Man* – an educated and cultured Jew who observed the **mitzvot** fully. The Israel Man should seek God both in the **Torah** and in nature.

He had a saying: 'Torah together with secular [non-religious] education'. He wrote many books, including a translation and commentary on the Five Books of Moses.

RABBI AZRIEL HILDSHEIMER (1820–1899)

In 1869 Rabbi Hildsheimer became rabbi of an Orthodox congregation in Berlin. He set up a seminary for training rabbis. He went further than Hirsch. He wanted to show that Judaism could work alongside modern culture. It could also cope with the critical scientific study of the classical Jewish texts. He also accepted non-Orthodox (see page 136) leaders in his seminary.

Some rabbis thought this was too much. However the Lithuanian **yeshivot** (see page 128) did not train rabbis, while the non-Orthodox academies did. Hildsheimer said that rabbis needed skills to cope in modern society.

Forty years later, a writer commented that it was the Rabbinical Seminary that enabled the traditional teachings of Judaism to survive in western Europe.

Today, Jews' College in London, Yeshiva University in New York and Bar Ilan University in Ramat Gan, Israel, are the direct result of Hildsheimer's work in setting up his seminary.

NEO-ORTHODOXY

Neo-Orthodoxy is the name given to the form of Judaism taught by Rabbis Hirsch and Hildsheimer. People who followed it accepted the authority of **Shulchan Aruch** (see page 32) and were strict in their observance of mitzvot. At the same time, they spoke German, wore western clothes and believed that secular (non-religious) studies should be part of the education of modern Jews. They also believed that women should be educated. Hirsch always insisted that it was possible to lead a full Jewish life in a non-Jewish society. To do this a person had to be totally committed to Judaism and to see art and science as tools for serving God.

During the 1930s many neo-Orthodox Jews escaped from Germany and settled in Britain, the USA and other countries. They taught the ideals of Hirsch in their communities. Neo-Orthodox ideas helped to form modern centrist Orthodox communities (see Unit 66).

FACTFILE

Jewish education BCE

The Bible stresses the importance of education. There is evidence to show that literacy was widespread in ancient Israel. There are many Biblical references to laws being written down and read to the people. The **Talmud** states there were schools for boys at the age of six. An early teacher said that 25 was the maximum number of boys who should be taught together. If there were more, an additional teacher should be employed.

QUOTE

The Jew will never frown at any art, any science, any culture…ready to accept whatever is true and good.

(Rabbi Samson Raphael Hirsch)

The three kinds of Orthodoxy described in Units 63–5 began as quite separate groups. They belonged to particular geographical areas. They did not want to have much to do with each other. Today, although most Hasidic groups tend to keep to themselves, they have all helped to create British Orthodoxy.

In Britain, Orthodoxy now has two main groups – 'centrist' and 'right-wing'. These are not entirely separate. They are two ways that Orthodox Jews express their religion.

Most centrist Orthodox families send their children to ordinary, non-Jewish schools. If they do choose Jewish schools, they would be ones that combine Jewish studies with a wide secular (non-religious) range of subjects.

Right-wing Orthodox families would only choose a Jewish school that put Jewish studies first.

THE GROWTH OF ORTHODOXY

During the first half of the twentieth century most Jews in Britain showed little interest in observing the Jewish religion (see page 12). In the late 1960s this began to change. There were three reasons for this.

- Firstly, the number of religious communities grew. There were new schools, synagogues, community centres, even a newspaper. Some Jews entered local and national politics.

- Secondly, following the **Holocaust** and the establishment of the State of Israel, Jews began to be more interested in their history and culture (see page 13).

- Finally, in June 1967 the Six Day War took place. Several Arab countries, led by President Nasser of Egypt, began a war against Israel (see page 63). In six days, Israel defeated them and the war was over.

Jews everywhere were shocked. Other countries, except for the United States, had stood silently by while Israel was attacked. Jews outside Israel realized they were alone. They looked to their own development, and made stronger links with Israel.

NEW DEVELOPMENTS IN BRITISH ORTHODOXY

The largest synagogue organization in Britain is the United Synagogue. It previously only took university graduates as **rabbis**. Now they accepted men with **yeshiva** training, mainly from Lithuanian-type yeshivot (see page 128).

There has been renewed interest in Jewish education. More families want to send their children to Jewish schools. Synagogues opened study groups. Businessmen take time to attend 'lunch and learn' sessions.

Habad Hasidim

Rabbi Menachem Mendel Schneerson (1902–1994) led **Habad Hasidim** to begin a series of campaigns to teach people about the **mitzvot**. From 1967 they established Habad houses, regional study centres in various parts of Britain.

Project Seed

Other Orthodox Jews provided one-to-one teaching to explain beliefs and practices to students. This was Project Seed. There were new translations of the **Tenakh**, **Mishnah**, **Midrash** and **Talmud**. Other new books included Jewish novels and children's books, including picture-books for toddlers.

Science and technology

There were new books on modern issues. For example, on the use of electricity on **Shabbat** (see page 40) and running a modern **kosher** kitchen. Rabbis began to specialize in technological issues. Scientists and doctors helped Jews to come to terms with the world today. The **halakhah** was seriously dealing with modern questions. Popular journals appeared (in English) so people could read about these developments.

ORTHODOXY TODAY

There are now about 300 Orthodox synagogues in Britain. Each belongs to one of four synagogue organizations. The Chief Rabbi is head of the largest group. There are new schools, yeshivot and seminaries, as well as youth movements. In London, Jews' College now trains yeshiva graduates in the skills they need to enable them to become rabbis. There is more demand for kosher food, so there are more kosher shops and restaurants. Family purity (see page 77) is being observed and there is a demand for new **mikvaot** (plural of mikveh).

HOW ORTHODOX JEWS SEE THEMSELVES

Orthodox Jews see themselves keeping the ancient traditions of Judaism in the modern world. They believe the **Torah** is the eternal will of God. They must live by this in the world of today, just as their ancestors lived by it in their day. This does not mean changing their religion. It means adjusting their lifestyles so that they can live according to the Torah. Sometimes problems arise. For example, finding jobs that will let them have time off for Shabbat and festivals, buying kosher food or praying with a **minyan** (see page 65). Orthodox Jews accept these as part of the discipline of living as Jews. They see themselves as serving God in every part of their lives.

HOW OTHERS SEE THEM

Non-Orthodox Jews (see Units 67–70) may think Orthodox Jews are making life hard for themselves. Some think they could live more easily by changing Judaism, as they have done (see page 138). They call right-wing Orthodox Jews 'fundamentalists' (this means someone who thinks the Torah is literally the word of God). They use this as a scornful term. They do not like the way that Orthodox Jews do not accept their practices, nor recognize their leaders as rabbis.

Prayer time in Bnei Akiva, an Orthodox youth movement

FACTFILE

Keeping kashrut

In the modern world, keeping kashrut has special importance for Orthodox Jews. It is something that helps them to keep their Jewish identity, and remember all the time their faithfulness to God. Worship is something that enters every part of their life – and kashrut is part of that worship. By keeping kashrut, Orthodox Jews worship even as they eat.

Non-Orthodox Jews do not believe that the **Torah** was literally given to Moses on Mount Sinai. They believe that Jewish beliefs and practices may be changed in order to allow Jews to fit in with modern society. Orthodox Jews do not consider that non-Orthodox groups teach true Judaism.

Non-Orthodox Jews are a minority in Britain. There are three main groups: Reform, Liberal and Masorti.

HOW THE REFORM MOVEMENT BEGAN

(Read Unit 4 before you begin this section.)

Unit 4 explains how the **maskilim** wanted to change the way Jews lived so that others would grant them full civil rights. In 1778 the first school opened in Berlin to give secular (non-religious) education to Jewish children. Soon, young Jews in Germany began to drift away from Jewish observance. They became German in their lifestyle and outlook. Some were baptized as Christians.

Others wanted to change the synagogue service to make it similar to church services. They thought this would raise the esteem of Judaism in the eyes of Germans. In 1810 Israel Jacobson founded a school at Seesen in Hanover. Jewish children were taught non-religious subjects there. He held services where there were songs and sermons in German as well as an organ, as in the church. Similar services began to take place in other towns.

In 1818 the Hamburg Temple was opened. This was the first Reform synagogue.

Soon there were more changes in different communities. Some used German for prayers and sang to organ accompaniment. Others abolished circumcision and moved **Shabbat** to Sunday. The most important change was in Jewish thinking. Some people began to believe that people could alter Judaism to suit their needs.

LEADERS

The Reform movement spread. Communities who had a majority who favoured it wanted leaders who thought as they did. New Reform groups also began to look for Reform **rabbis**.

Men who were chosen as rabbis in the reforming communities did not have the traditional background. Mainly they were German-Jewish scholars. They had been trained in the universities, rather than the **yeshivot** (see page 89).

The most outstanding men of the Reform movement were Samuel Hirsch (1815–1889) and Samuel Holdheim (1806–1860). Hirsch (no relation to Samuel Raphael Hirsh, see page 132) taught that the **mitzvot** were merely symbols of God's teaching. When people's lives changed, then the symbols (i.e. the mitzvot) could be thrown out. This was because the symbols did not have the same meanings any more. Holdheim saw the mitzvot as something that belonged to the ancient Jewish state that was destroyed by the Romans nearly 2000 years earlier. Holdheim said this made the mitzvot out-of-date.

Abraham Geiger

Abraham Geiger (1810–1874)

Abraham Geiger was the most influential teacher in the early Reform movement. He felt at home in Germany and had no great desire to return to the Holy Land (see page 24). He taught that the Jews were a religious community, not a nation. He saw no need to pray for the restoration of a Jewish state.

Geiger showed how Judaism had changed. He said that Judaism had always had to change to suit new conditions. The rabbis of the Middle Ages had remodelled the Judaism of the Talmudic period. The rabbis of the **Talmud** had adapted the Judaism of Biblical times. Therefore, he believed, it was reasonable for modern rabbis to remodel Judaism yet again. Geiger believed that Judaism could be seen as 'ethical monotheism'. That is, belief in One God linked to high standards of moral behaviour. He said the only mitzvot that had value were those that led to this ideal. Other mitzvot were no longer binding and could be forgotten.

OPPOSITION AND EXPANSION

Rabbis in Germany and elsewhere opposed these changes. They were afraid the Reform movement would divide the Jewish people by setting up a separate community. They did all they could to persuade the German authorities to close down the Reform synagogues. However, most rabbis did not have a university education and were no match for the reformers. The only one who successfully opposed the reformers was Rabbi Samson Raphael Hirsch (see page 132). He argued so well for Torah-true Judaism that even Geiger admired him.

The Reform movement spread through Germany and the Netherlands to other European countries. It reached the United States in 1824. Reform began in Britain in 1842 when the West London Synagogue was formed.

REFORM CONFERENCES

Between 1844 and 1871 the Reform leaders held a number of conferences to decide what Reform Judaism should believe and practice.

They felt they were part of German society and did not wish to leave Europe. They stopped praying for the restoration of the Holy Land and the rebuilding of the Temple (see page 24). They gave up believing in the physical coming of a messiah. They reinterpreted this to mean a hope that there would be a messianic age. This would be a time when there would be universal peace and God's presence would be felt throughout the world. They also decided the food laws (see page 68) could be set aside. They discussed many other topics, including the status of women, and the meaning of 'work' on Shabbat.

FACTFILE

Bromley Synagogue, Kent

Bromley Synagogue (Reform) began life as a church that was converted into four small flats. In the late 1960s a group of Jewish families got together to buy the old church. They pulled down the flats inside and soon they had their own synagogue. Nearly all its fittings and fixtures were made by members of the congregation. Now many of the congregation come from different parts of south London, but they all feel as though they are part of one community.

Today the USA has the largest number of Reform congregations. American Reform is more like the Liberal movement in Britain (see Unit 69). Reform in Britain has only grown in the last thirty years or so.

Early in the twentieth century, British Reform was concerned that worship should be orderly and dignified. As it grew its leaders became more involved in education and youth activities and teaching a more positive view of Israel. Now it has forty synagogues in Britain. They belong to the Reform Synagogues of Great Britain (RSGB) which was founded in 1942.

REFORM PRACTICE

The synagogue

Services vary, but some parts are fixed. Prayers are shorter than in Orthodox synagogues and some may be in English. The prayer for a return to the Holy Land and the rebuilding of the Temple is left out.

Men and women sit together in Reform synagogues. Women may carry the **Torah** scrolls to and from the Ark and are called to recite blessings. Girls may read from the Torah at their **bat mitzvah**. There are some women **rabbis**. **Tefillin** are not always worn.

Shabbat

Traditionally, **Shabbat** always started at sunset on Friday (see page 37). Reform families light the candles and begin Shabbat at any time on Friday evening. Also, they regard 'work' not as the 39 **melachot**, but as paid work.

Reform Jews often drive cars on Shabbat. This is usually to attend synagogue or visit friends and family. They also use electrical appliances. They observe festivals in a similar way, but do not observe the 'second day' of some festivals.

Marriage and divorce

The marriage ceremony is traditional, but the laws of 'family purity' (see page 77) are not followed.

Women in Reform synagogues may carry the Torah scrolls

There are two ways of obtaining a divorce. One involves the traditional giving of a **get** (see page 78). If a husband refuses to give a get, the Reform **bet din** issues a document that dissolves the marriage. Reform and Liberal congregations accept this. However for Orthodox Jews there may be the problem of **mamzerut** (see page 79).

The dietary laws

Reform homes are not as strict about **kashrut** as Orthodox homes, though they keep some of the laws. Synagogues officially have **kosher** catering.

Sexual matters

Reform groups consider contraception and abortion from a medical or social point of view. Their leaders accept homosexuality (see page 110) as an acceptable alternative lifestyle.

Death and mourning

Reform communities observe the saying of **kaddish**, but they do not tear their garments (see page 80). They do not always keep the full week of **shiva**. Some will cremate bodies if the family asks for it.

Conversion

Orthodox conversion is explained on page 23. Reform conversion did not require immersion until 1980. However, Reform groups recognize as Jewish anyone who was accepted before then. Orthodox Jews do not recognize Reform conversion as valid.

Zionism

Early reformers thought of themselves as loyal Germans or Americans. They did not look to a Jewish homeland in Palestine. They thought the dispersion of Jews throughout the world was not a punishment for sin. They thought it was God's way of bringing Jews into contact with other people so that they could work for a better world (see page 99). The Pittsburgh Platform of American Reform (1885) states:

> 'We consider ourselves…a religious community, and…expect neither a return to Palestine…nor the restoration of any of the laws concerning the Jewish state.'

However, while Reform congregations no longer pray for a return to **Zion**, most do pray for the welfare of Israel.

HOW MEMBERS OF REFORM SEE THEMSELVES

Reform Synagogues of Great Britain have the slogan 'Rooted in the past, responding to change'. Many members see Reform as a modernized form of Judaism. Others attend Reform synagogues because they like to pray in English, or to sit together as a family.

One problem for Reform members is about the authority of the rabbi. As the Reform movement teaches that the Torah is not literally the word of God, the rabbi's authority cannot rest on the Torah. So why should people follow his teaching?

Claude Montefiore, a Liberal Jew (see Unit 69) said it all depended on individual conscience. Reform leaders have not really solved the problem.

A second problem concerns the Reform attitude to Jewish laws and practices. After much debate, they decided that 'ceremonial' laws (about how worship should be conducted) could be abolished, but moral laws could not. Today RSGB states, 'We follow tradition unless there are religious or ethical reasons for departing from its practice'.

HOW OTHERS SEE THEM

Orthodox Jews see Reform Jews as a watered-down form of Judaism. They are concerned about the number of converts who they do not recognize as Jewish. Mainly they are concerned about the split in the community caused by Reform observing a different definition of Judaism.

FACTFILE

Women in Judaism

Reform Judaism allows women to take a much greater part in synagogues and to hold high office within the Jewish community. For example, in September 1972 Sally Preisand became the first female rabbi in Reform Judaism. Today many non-Orthodox synagogues have female rabbis. Women also hold high political office.

QUOTE

Blessed art Thou, O Lord our God, King of the Universe,
Who has chosen us from all people and given us Thy Law…
(Blessing on removing the Torah from the Ark)

The Liberal movement began in Britain through the work of Lily Montagu and Claude Montefiore. People thought the Reform movement was too strict, and more changes were needed.

LILY MONTAGU (1873–1963)

Lily Montagu was a social worker among poor immigrant families. She saw their struggle to make a living, and their anxiety about having to work on **Shabbat** (see page 12). She felt that Judaism should change to make it easier for them. In 1902 she and Claude Montefiore founded the Jewish Religious Union. This became the Union of Liberal and Progressive Synagogues. There are now 29 Liberal congregations in Britain.

Claude Montefiore

CLAUDE MONTEFIORE (1858–1938)

Claude Montefiore was a member of a Reform congregation. He thought that it was difficult for people to follow the kind of Judaism it taught. He also believed the ethical teachings of Christianity were better than those of Judaism. He wanted people to have choices in their religion. He developed the idea of 'the enlightened consciousness'. He meant that people should study the traditional beliefs, then choose what they wanted to keep.

LIBERAL BELIEFS

Montefiore taught that God did not *literally* reveal himself to Moses at Mount Sinai nor to the prophets. Rather, people become aware of the presence of God as He makes Himself felt in their consciousness (or mind).

This led to the Liberal view that observing **mitzvot** is a matter of personal choice. Some people may need to observe mitzvot as a personal discipline, to develop their moral character. For example, eating **kosher** food (see page 68) may be a moral discipline for those who want it. But it is not binding on all members. Liberal Jews can feel free to follow whatever practices they have chosen.

Leaders of the Liberal movement have been troubled by the **Holocaust** (see page 16). They ask how God could have allowed it to happen? Some try to account for this by suggesting that God is not all-powerful (see page 18). They suggest that God himself, like humans, struggles to overcome evil.

LIBERAL PRACTICE

Although members have a great deal of choice in their religious observance, similar practices can be found in most Liberal congregations in Britain.

The synagogue

Prayers are similar to those in Reform synagogues. Men and women sit together and men need not wear a hat or kippah. Boys and girls can be 'confirmed' at sixteen in Liberal synagogues. This takes place at **Shavuot**.

Sabbaths and festivals

Liberal families do not have to start Sabbaths and festivals at sunset (see page 37). They may light the candles when it suits them. Some festival practices, like lighting the **Hanukkah** lamp (see page 56), blowing the **shofar** on **Rosh Hashanah** (see page 45) and fasting on **Yom Kippur** (see page 46) still happen. On **Pesach**, Liberal families eat **matzah** (see page 50) but do not have to buy '**kosher** for Passover' foods. They do not fast on **Tisha b'Av** (see page 60) or other fast days. They do not believe the **Torah** was given on Mount Sinai, so Shavuot (see page 52) has only symbolic meaning.

Marriage

In the marriage ceremony in a Liberal synagogue both the groom and the bride say, 'With this ring you are sanctified to me…' (see page 77). Both respond to the questions in English, 'Do you take this man…?' 'Do you take this woman…?' The ceremony takes place under a **huppah** (see page 76).

Divorce

There is no Liberal divorce procedure and no **get**. Liberal congregations accept civil divorces as valid. Orthodox Jews feel that a woman remarrying without a get may cause future children to be **mamzerim** (see page 79). Liberal leaders sometimes suggest a divorcing couple should arrange a get through the Orthodox authorities.

Mourning

For Liberal Jews the seven-day mourning period (**shiva**) is optional. They may choose a burial in a plain coffin, or cremation. **Kaddish** is recited on Friday night.

Who is a Jew?

Traditionally a child is Jewish only if its mother is Jewish. The Liberal movement regards a child as Jewish if either parent is a Jew. Any person raised as a Jew (e.g. an adopted child) is also considered to be Jewish. This is provided the child was under seven years of age when adopted. If the child of a Jewish mother was brought up in another faith, Liberals would regard him or her as a non-Jew.

Life after death

Liberal Jews do not believe in a bodily resurrection (see page 24). They have removed all references to it from their prayer book. Many believe that the soul is immortal (never dies). Some do not believe this. They feel that we are only immortal as long as future generations remember us.

FACTFILE

Confirmation

Liberal Jews dropped **bar/bat mitzvah** in the 1800s. Instead they had confirmation at sixteen (see opposite). Many Liberal Jews today have a bat/bar mitzvah at age twelve or thirteen *and* confirmation at sixteen. Many young adults feel that at twelve or thirteen they were not really mature enough to make a proper commitment. At sixteen they feel they are more sensible and can take on responsibility for their religious duties.

The Liberal movement came about because people felt that Reform had not gone far enough. Masorti felt Reform had gone too far.

MASORTI ANCESTRY

The Assembly of Masorti Synagogues is the youngest non-Orthodox movement in the UK. It began in 1991. It is based on the teachings of German Reform thinkers such as Zacharias Frankel (1801–1875). He did not agree with the ideas of Geiger, Holdheim and others (see page 136). He believed that Judaism had always changed to suit new circumstances and that slight changes could be good. His ideas are the basis of the Conservative movement in the USA. Masorti is the British equivalent.

MASORTI BELIEFS

In 1957 Dr Louis Jacobs, **rabbi** of the (Orthodox) North West End Synagogue, wrote a book. In it he said that God did not give the **Torah** at Mount Sinai (see page 6). He said Judaism was the result of people's religious experiences. He said that God revealed himself in the world that humans live in. The Bible is composed of stories of personal encounters with God in the history of the Jewish people.

According to him, the Torah is made up of writings from different times and places. There were many authors, who described how they thought they were experiencing God. The Torah is special because Jews have always seen God at work within it. This makes it different from other ancient writings.

In 1963 Dr Jacobs left Orthodoxy and set up an independent synagogue. From this congregation the Masorti movement grew.

Masorti believe that the Torah is not literally God's word. This means that **halakhah** is not related to the actual words of the Torah. They say halakhah relates to the Torah's ideas. Some rabbis developed halakhot from actual words – even unusual spellings of

Dr Louis Jacobs

words – in the Torah (see page 30). If they were mistaken, this suggests their halakhot should no longer apply.

Dr Jacobs said it does not matter how the halakhot came about. What does matter is that the laws and customs 'have all contributed to the ennoblement of Jewish life and the elevation of the Jewish spirit'. This means that the **mitzvot** have become holy because Jews have observed them for so long as a way of serving God. They do not regard mitzvot as God's actual commands.

MASORTI PRACTICE

The synagogue service

Masorti services generally follow those in Orthodox synagogues, with some variations. Some have separate seating for men and women (see page 84). Others are like the Reform, and have mixed seating. Some let women read from the Torah, and count them as part of a **minyan** (see page 91).

The dietary laws

Masorti members observe parts of **kashrut**, e.g. regarding meat and fish. They do not insist on other things such as **kosher** wine.

Conversions

Masorti require circumcision for male converts and immersion in a **mikveh** for both men and women. They accept Reform converts who converted after 1980 (see page 138). Anyone who converted before then has to be immersed. They do not accept Liberal conversions. Orthodox authorities do not accept Masorti conversions as valid.

Marriage and divorce

These follow traditional practice. Marriage takes place under a **huppah** and divorce requires the giving of a **get**. Masorti do not recognize Reform and Liberal divorce procedures. However, Orthodox authorities do not recognize Masorti marriages.

Zionism

Masorti support Zionism (see page 144) but members do not pray for the rebuilding of the Temple. They do not regard Israel as a holy land in itself. Rather, holiness lies in the prayers and hopes of the Jewish people directed towards Israel.

HOW MASORTI SEE THEMSELVES

Masorti leaders claim to 'maintain the laws and practices of the past as far as possible' while believing that the Torah is not the actual word of God. They believe they preserve the halakhah in a way that Reform does not. Members believe their movement offers an Orthodox style of Judaism without the outdated beliefs.

HOW OTHERS SEE THEM

Orthodox leaders do not accept that Masorti maintain the laws and practices of the past. This is proved by the way that Masorti allow mixed seating in the synagogues and count women in the minyan; also by not accepting that the Torah is the actual word of God. They say that Masorti is the thin end of the wedge that can bring in unlimited change.

They point to the way that the Conservative movement in the USA began with largely traditional practices. However, by the 1930s young men who were not sympathetic to tradition came to the leadership. The movement began to change traditional practices. Since the 1940s it has begun to copy the American Reform movement. It no longer observes the second day of festivals (see page 48). It allows the use of electrical appliances on **Shabbat**, and has brought its divorce procedure more in line with that of the Reform movement.

FACTFILE

The smallest Jewish group?

The Samaritans regard themselves as true Jews, faithful only to the Torah and the book of Joshua. There are two Samaritan communities today, each of about 300 people. One group is in the Jewish town of Holon and one in the Arab town of Shechem. They speak Arabic, but worship in an ancient form of Hebrew.

'…the members of the National Council, representing the Jewish people in Palestine…hereby proclaim the establishment of the Jewish State in Palestine, to be called Israel.'

(Israel's Declaration of Independence, May 1948)

Zion was once another name for Jerusalem. For many Jews it meant the whole of the Holy Land. Zionism is the belief that Palestine should be the Jewish homeland. The Zionist movement worked for and achieved a Jewish homeland in Palestine. Today it supports the State of Israel.

THE ORIGINS OF ZIONISM

Three things led to the forming of the Zionist movement:

- the traditional Jewish hope for a return to their homeland
- the rise of nationalism during the nineteenth century
- **anti-semitism**.

The hope for a return

In the Bible God said to Abraham, 'I will give this land to your descendants' (*Genesis 12:7*). He repeated this promise to Isaac and Jacob. He warned them that if they sinned they would be driven out of their land for a time (*Leviticus 26:33–45*). The prophets said they would one day return (*Amos 9:14–15*).

In time, the Jews were scattered over the world. However, always a few remained in Israel. For nearly 2000 years Jews prayed every day that God would give them back their land.

The rise of nationalism

From the Middle Ages onwards, many wars were fought in Europe. This resulted in many changes in national boundaries. Toward the end of the eighteenth century people became more involved in their own culture. They wanted new nation-states where people were related to each other by race and language. This was nationalism.

Many Jews, too, especially the younger generation, began to think of having their own state. Some began to look to Palestine for a Jewish homeland, a Jewish nation-state. At that time Palestine was ruled by the Turks.

Anti-semitism

Nationalism in Europe affected Jews badly. Where states were created on a racial basis, the rights of people of a different race were restricted. Anti-semitism is hatred of Jews. Jews were a target for hatred in France, Germany and Austria. Jews who regarded themselves as loyal French or German citizens were shocked.

In 1881 there were **pogroms** (anti-Jewish riots) in Russia, and 160 Jewish communities suffered death and destruction (see page 15). In 1882 the Tsarist Government passed the May Laws that restricted Jewish business. This ruined many Jewish family businesses. Many Jews felt unwanted, and some emigrated to Britain (see page 12), the USA and South Africa. Others looked towards Palestine where the **Hovovei Zion** (lovers of Zion) supported people who wanted to settle there.

HIBAT ZION (LOVE OF ZION)

Soon Jews in Russia and Romania formed societies to send Jews to Palestine. Wealthy Jews supported this work, and founded a settlement in 1874. This was a very small-scale programme. There was no political organization or leadership until Dr Pinsker arrived.

Y L PINSKER (1821–1891)

Yehuda Leib (Leon) Pinsker was a doctor living in Odessa (see page 15). He believed that Jews should accept Russian culture and take up gentile (non-Jewish) ways. He changed his mind because of the pogroms and the Tsarist

Government's anti-semitism. He felt that anti-semitism occurred because Jews were always seen as foreigners. In 1882 he wrote a book, *Autoemancipation*, in which he said that if the Jews had a country of their own there would be no need for anti-semitism.

The Hovovei Zion welcomed his book. They invited Dr Pinsker to set up a committee to build settlements in Palestine. They met in Kattowitz in Germany in 1884. He was chosen as head of this new committee and began to travel to raise funds. The Jews were expelled from Moscow in 1891 and Hovovei Zion sent more people to Palestine. However, the Turkish authorities stopped immigration and Hovovei Zion ran out of money. Dr Pinsker died before any firm plans could be made.

◇

FACTFILE

Flowing with milk and honey

Although a small country, much of it arid desert or hostile mountains, Israel is able to produce enough food for its own people and for export.

South of the Dead Sea is the Arava, Israel's grasslands. Israeli farmers have learned to get the maximum possible use from the least possible amount of water. Despite average annual rainfall of less than one inch (25 mm) and summer temperatures of 40°C, they are able to produce out-of-season fruit and vegetables, mainly for export. In the north, the Jesreel valley produces a wide variety of fruits and vegetables. Israeli oranges are famous worldwide, as are its capsicum (peppers), avocados and soft fruits.

The Kattowitz conference. Dr Pinsker is in the front row, centre. On his right is Rabbi Mohilever (see page 148)

THEODOR HERZL (1850–1904)

'If you will it, it is no idle dream.'

(Theodor Herzl)

Herzl was an Austrian journalist. In 1895 he was in Paris to report on the trial of Alfred Dreyfus, a Jewish officer in the French army. Dreyfus was falsely accused of treason (see page 15). This triggered a wave of **anti-semitism** as the French Government said the Jews were responsible. The mob began to shout, 'Death to the Jews.' Herzl asked a fellow journalist how such a thing could happen in a civilized country. 'They are enjoying the shaming of a Jew,' he replied.

The Dreyfus trial affected Herzl deeply. He concluded that anti-semitism was unavoidable. It was because people hated strangers. It would go on until Jews had a land of their own. This became his passion, and he spent the rest of his life working to bring this about.

First he went to wealthy Jews known for their willingness to help others. They did not take him seriously. Then he put his ideas in writing. In 1896 he published a pamphlet, 'Der Judenstaat' ('The Jewish State'). In it he said that anti-semitism was a fact of life. Jews could only avoid it if they had their own land in which to settle. He said there should be a Society of Jews to represent the Jewish people, and a Jewish Company to arrange finance. Then they could buy land in Palestine or Argentina, and Jews could begin to move.

Many Jews felt quite at home in western Europe so they rejected Herzl's ideas (see page 136). Religious Jews objected (their reasons are explained in Unit 73). Western **Hovovei Zion** thought his scheme was too ambitious. However, eastern Hovovei Zion eagerly received his plan and proposed Herzl as their leader. In August 1897, Herzl set up the first Zionist congress in Basle, Switzerland, which agreed to create a home for the Jewish people in Palestine, guaranteed by public law.

Herzl began to meet heads of state and other important people to ask them to support his ideas. It was only in Britain that he had some success. In 1902 Joseph Chamberlain, a British government minister, suggested a Jewish settlement in Uganda. Herzl thought this might be a first step to getting land in Palestine. However, the next Zionist Congress rejected the plan. The Jewish homeland had to be in Palestine.

THE BRITISH MANDATE

In 1900 the World Zionist Organization set up the Jewish National Fund to buy land in Palestine. The Fund was based in London. Tel Aviv, the first modern Jewish city, was founded in 1909 on land purchased by the Fund. In 1917 the British Government, having spoken to President Wilson of the USA, gave its support for a Jewish homeland in Palestine. This was written in a letter that became known as the 'Balfour Declaration' (see below).

Foreign Office
November 2nd, 1917

Dear Lord Rothschild,

I have much pleasure in conveying to you… the following declaration…

'His Majesty's Government view with favour the establishment in Palestine of a national home for the Jewish people, and [will do their best to bring this about]. It must be clearly understood that [this will not affect] the civil and religious rights of existing non-Jewish communities in Palestine, or…of Jews in any other country.'…

Yours sincerely,

Arthur James Balfour

A month later General Allenby brought Palestine under British control. Three years later Britain accepted the Mandate of Palestine. They agreed to help set up a homeland for Jewish people in Palestine.

THE STATE IS BORN

By the end of World War II in 1945, thousands of **Holocaust** survivors urgently needed resettlement (see page 16). Many tried to get into Palestine. For political reasons the British forces were told to turn back the refugee ships. Some of the ships were old and sank after being turned back. Thousands of Jews who had survived the Nazi death camps now drowned. Jewish resistance movements began to attack British military targets. The Arabs, who did not want the Jews there, also attacked. In 1947 the United Nations voted to split Palestine into separate Arab and Jewish states. On 14 May 1948 the State of Israel was established.

KEY WORD

Mandate – when one country is given authority to rule over another, as when Britain ruled Palestine

FACTFILE

El Al

The name of Israel's airline is El Al. This is taken from a passage in **Nevi'im** (see page 28) in the book of *Ezekiel*. Ezekiel tells of a time in the future when all Jews will be gathered together to return to their Holy Land. He uses the phrase, in Hebrew, 'el al' which means 'upward'. He prophesied, ' I will take the people of Israel from the nations among which they have gone, and will gather them from all sides, and bring them to their own land.' (*Ezekiel 37:21*)

14 May 1948. David Ben-Gurion declares the State of Israel

Zionism was a problem for religious Jews. They had hoped and prayed for a return to the Holy Land for many centuries. But now the return was being achieved by secular (non-religious) Jews – many of whom actually rejected Judaism.

RELIGIOUS ZIONISM

Rabbi Shmuel Mohilever (1824–1898)

After the **pogroms** of 1881, **Rabbi** Mohilever thought that Jews escaping from Russia should settle in Palestine. He supported the ideal of **Hibat Zion** (see page 144). He became President of the Kattowitz conference of 1884 (see page 145). He used the account of Ezekiel's vision of a valley of dry bones that joined together and came alive again (*Ezekiel 37*) as a symbol for the renewal of Jewish life in the Holy Land.

At a meeting of **Hovovei Zion** in 1893, he tried to persuade other Orthodox people to join the movement. This was to make sure the new Jewish settlements would be religious. This led to the forming of the Mizrahi movement.

The Mizrahi movement

In 1902 Rabbi Yitzhak Reines (1839–1915) founded the Mizrahi movement, an organization of religious Zionists.

The Mizrahi wanted to ensure the future of Judaism through the study of the **Torah**, observance of the **mitzvot** and return to the Holy Land. In 1920 the World Zionist Organization made Mizrahi responsible for Jewish education in Palestine. This continued until 1953. The next year Rabbi Avraham Yitzhak Kook became Chief Rabbi of Palestine (see opposite).

The Mizrahi movement worked hard to keep the Jewish character of the State of Israel. Due to its efforts, **Shabbat** is an official day of rest when no public transport runs. In addition, Israeli soldiers are provided with **kosher** food. Mizrahi also set up a Ministry of Religions. They also kept marriage and divorce in the hands of the rabbis.

Rabbi Avraham Yitzhak Kook (1865–1935)

Rabbi Kook criticized the World Zionist Organization for concentrating only on the non-religious, cultural needs of Jews. He also criticized Mizrahi for not properly explaining religious Zionism. For him, the return of Jews to the land promised to them was 'the beginning of the Messianic redemption' (see page 24). He meant that the return of the Jews to **Zion** (the Holy Land) was the first step towards a time of universal peace. Then the Messiah would enable all people to become aware of God in the world. He believed that the **Sanhedrin** (see page 30)

Rabbi Avraham Yitzhak Kook

would soon be restored now that there was a Chief Rabbi in Jerusalem.

Rabbi Kook was concerned that the return to the Holy Land had been brought about by mainly non-religious Zionists. However, he felt it was possible to do God's work without realizing it. He thought the most non-religious person was doing God's will by rebuilding the Holy Land. He thought that the Zionists' sense of commitment to the Jewish people would lead them back to a spiritual awareness.

For Rabbi Kook, Jewish nationality did not depend on country or language and culture. Jewish nationality was God-given. It was not Jews led by Zionists who chose to settle in the Holy Land – it was God's plan.

RELIGIOUS OPPOSITION TO ZIONISM

Many rabbis in eastern and central Europe at first disapproved of the Hovovei Zion and the Zionist movement. This was because:

- they believed that the Messiah (see page 24) would bring about the return to Zion and Jews had to wait for this
- they felt that Zionism would weaken Jewish values and religion because its leaders were not religious.

They pointed out how Pinsker, his closest friend Moshe Lilienblum, and even Herzl, had all at some time supported the idea that Jews should give up their religion and become more like non-Jews. Hertzl had indeed proposed a Jewish state without any reference to religion. His idea was a Jewish state where rabbis would stay in their synagogues and the rest of the people would live non-religious lives. The main opposition came from **Agudat Yisrael** (Union of Israel), an Orthodox group who wanted to protect the authority of the rabbis.

Agudat Yisrael objected to religious Jews working with non-religious Zionists. They did not accept the idea of a non-religious Jewish state in the Holy Land. If it was not run according to the Torah, it could not be a Jewish state.

When the Nazis came to power, Agudat Yisrael began co-operating with the World Zionist Organization. However they still refused to call the homeland a Jewish state.

FACTFILE

Minorities in Israel

Over five million people live in Israel today. About one million of these are non-Jews. They are mainly Arabic-speaking. About 750 000 are Muslim, most of whom are Sunni. About 70 000 of the Muslim Arabs are Bedouin, from about 30 tribes. There are also 150 000 Christians and 80 000 **Druse**.

Israel today is a modern democracy. Like other countries it has cities, factories, farms, schools, hospitals and universities. It has all the modern features you would expect. And like other countries it has social problems such as crime, unemployment and drug addiction. But there are some features that are special because it is a Jewish state.

A JEWISH STATE

Israel's population is very mixed. The great majority are Jews, but some are religious and others are not. Some even think Judaism now has no useful purpose for those who live in Israel. Religious Jews feel that Israel gives them the opportunity to observe Judaism in a way that Jews living in the **diaspora** cannot.

These two ways of thinking sometimes cause rows – but these are usually verbal. When it comes to defending Israel, religious and non-religious Israelis have fought and died for one another.

Judaism is the official religion of Israel. However, other faiths have their rights and their holy places are protected. Marriage and divorce are controlled by the **rabbis**. Non-religious Israelis do not like this, but it helps to prevent the risk of **mamzerim** (see page 79). Other laws are based on British law. Some parts of Jewish law are gradually being introduced into the system.

The Israeli flag has two horizontal blue stripes on a white background. This is like a huge **tallit** (see page 86). In the centre of the flag is a blue **Magen David**, a six-pointed 'Star of David'. No one knows where the Magan David came from, but it is a symbol of Judaism. During the **Holocaust** (see page 16), Jews had to wear the star on their clothing. You can see the Israeli flag in the picture on page 63.

KIBBUTZIM AND MOSHAVIM

Small towns and villages in Israel are either kibbutzim (singular **kibbutz**) or moshavim (singular **moshav**). Most are farming communities, but some have light industry.

Kibbutzim are collective settlements where no one owns private property. People joining a kibbutz hand over their belongings, but they can have them back if they leave. Everything is owned by the kibbutz. The members work for the benefit of the whole kibbutz.

Kibbutz meals are taken together. The laundry, hairdresser, clinic and clothes store are shared. But kibbutzim differ from place to place. Some even raise children together. They take their meals together and meet their parents at regular times. Others allow more individuality. Some kibbutzim are religious, but most are not.

In moshavim people own their own property.

ISRAEL AND THE DIASPORA

Jews in the diaspora have always contributed to funds for resettlement projects in Palestine. Today fund-raising still goes on to support **aliyah**. Aliyah means 'going to settle in Israel'.

At one time, many Israelis thought all Jews should go to live in Israel. Today some resent the funds being raised on Israel's behalf. However, for many non-religious Jews in the diaspora, giving money to Israel may be their only way of expressing their commitment to the Jewish people.

Israel today is a refuge for Jews anywhere in the world. One of the first laws the **Knesset** (Israel's Parliament) passed was the Law of Return. This gives every Jew the right to settle in Israel.

PILGRIMAGE

In Biblical times, Jews used to take regular offerings to the Temple (see page 48). This stopped when the Temple was destroyed (see page 8). Today Jews do not make pilgrimages as a religious duty. However, many Jews visit holy places in Israel and feel a sense of personal pilgrimage.

The Western Wall (Hakotel Hamaaravi)

This is the last wall of the Temple that is left standing. It is Judaism's most holy site. Jews used to visit it to pray and mourn the loss of the Temple. This gave it the name the Wailing Wall. From 1848 until the Six Day War in 1967 the Jordanians occupied Jerusalem, so Jews could not visit the Wall. Now there are services there every day. On festivals it is crowded. Boys come to celebrate their **bar mitzvah** (see page 74) at the Wall.

Yad Vashem

This is the **Holocaust** memorial in Jerusalem. It is described on page 62.

The tombs of great people

Maarat Hamachpelah in Hebron is the tomb of Abraham and Sarah, Isaac and Rebecca, Jacob and Leah. Tradition says Adam and Eve are buried there, too. It is in Arab territory, but they look after the tomb as Abraham is also their ancestor. Rachel, Jacob's second wife, is buried near Bet Lechem. Jews visit these tombs and pray there.

RELIGIOUS ATTITUDES TO ISRAEL TODAY

Religious Jews are glad that **yeshivot** (see page 89) and seminaries (see page 90) are successful in Israel with even more students than in the days of the Lithuanian yeshivot (see page 128). They are glad, too, that Jews can visit and pray at Judaism's holy places, and that Jews anywhere in the world can come to Israel if they are persecuted. However, they are very sad about things like crime and prostitution in Israel. They are upset by the sale of pork in some Israeli restaurants. They are offended when non-religious Israelis make fun of Judaism.

Usually they try to ignore the bad things and focus on the good things that come from having a Jewish state. After all, they are all members of the worldwide Jewish family.

Prayers at the Western Wall

FACTFILE

The land of Israel

Israel is a very small country – about the same size as Wales, but longer and narrower. It measures 290 miles (470 km) from north to south, and about 85 miles (135 km) across at its widest point. Its highest point is Mount Hermon, over 4000 feet (1200 m) high. Its lowest point, on the shores of the Dead Sea, is 1300 feet (400 m) below sea level.

GLOSSARY

Most words in this glossary are in Hebrew, the language of the Tenakh and the Mishnah. Today, modern Hebrew is the official language of Israel. Some of the Tenakh and most of the Talmud are written in Aramaic, a language related to Hebrew.

Some words are in Yiddish, a language similar to German. This was spoken by European Jews. Today it is not so common, but is still spoken in Hasidic communities (see page 130). Some Yeshivot (see page 89) teach in Yiddish.

Try to pronounce the words correctly. The part of the word printed in bold shows where to put the stress. Whenever you see 'ch' in these words, it should be pronounced like the Scottish 'loch' or the Welsh 'bach'.

Afikomen (*A'fee'koo'***man**) 'Dessert', the portion of matzah eaten at the end of the seder meal at Pesach (Passover)

Agadah (*A'ga'***dah**) A branch of Jewish teaching that shows how to relate Bible verses to beliefs and practices

Agudat Yisrael (*A'gu'***dat** *Yis'ra'***el**) 'Union of Israel'. An Orthodox group who wanted to restore the authority of the rabbis and Torah in Jewish life

Agunah (*A'gu'***nah**) A 'chained wife', a woman whose husband is missing but not known to be dead

Aleinu (*A'***lay**'*nu*) The final prayer in each synagogue service

Aliyah (*Al'i'***yah**) 1. Being called to recite a blessing over the Torah reading in the synagogue. 2. Going to settle in Israel

Amen (*Ah'***men**) 'Truly', said at the end of a blessing.

Anti-semitism Hatred of Jews

Aravot (*A'ra'***vot**) Branches of willow used during the festival of Sukkot

Arba'at haminim (*Ar'ba'***at** *ha'mi'***nim**) 'The four species' i.e. the four plants (palm, citron, myrtle and willow) used during Sukkot

Aron hakodesh (*A'***ron** *ha'ko'***desh**) The holy Ark, a curtained recess in the synagogue where the Torah scrolls are kept

Arvit (*Ar'***vit**) The evening service

Asarah b'Tevet (*A'sa'***ra** *be'***te**'*vet*) The 10th Tevet, a fast to mark the day the Babylonians laid siege to Jerusalem in 587 BCE

Ashkenazim (*Ash'ke'na'***zim**) Western Jews

Av Fifth month of the Jewish year (July/August)

Avel (*A'***vel**, pl. *A've'***lim**) A mourner (see also onan)

Bar Kokhba (**Bar** *kokh'***ba**) A Jewish leader who rebelled against the Romans in 132 CE

Bar mitzvah (**Bar** *mitz'***vah**) 'Son of the commandments', a boy who reaches Jewish adulthood at age thirteen

Baruch shepatarani (*Ba'***ruch** *she'pa'ta'***ra**'*ni*) The father of the boy or girl reaching adulthood declares they are now responsible for their own actions

Bat chayil (**Bat chay**'*il*) 'Daughter of excellence', a ceremony for girls reaching the age of twelve

Bat mitzvah (**Bat** *mitz'***vah**) 'Daughter of the commandments', a girl who reaches Jewish adulthood at age twelve

Bedikat chametz (*Be'dee'***kat** *cha'***metz**) The search for leaven (risen bread) on the evening before Passover

Bemidbar (*Bemid'***bar**) Hebrew for the Biblical Book of Numbers

Bereshit (*B'ray'***shit**) Hebrew for the Biblical Book of Genesis

Bet din (*Bet* **din**) 'House of Justice', a Jewish court of law

Bet din hagadol (*Bet* **din** *ha'ga'***dol**) 'Great House of Justice', the supreme Jewish court in ancient times

Bet ha Knesset (*Bet hak'***ness**'*et*) 'House of Assembly', Hebrew name for a synagogue

Bimah (*Bee'***mah**) Raised platform in a synagogue where the Torah is read

Birchat eirusin (*Bir'***chat** *ey'roo'***sin**) 'Blessings of betrothal', the first blessings at a wedding

Birchat nisuin (*Bir'***chat** *nis'oo'***in**) 'Blessings of marriage', the final blessings at a marriage

Blech Yiddish for 'tin', a metal sheet placed over a cooker on Sabbaths, so that saucepans can be moved around without being lifted

Brit milah (*Brit mee'***lah**) Covenant of circumcision

Challot (*Cha'***lot**) Special loaves of bread for Sabbaths and festivals

Chamesh Megillot (*Cha'***mesh** *Me'gi'***lot**) 'The five scrolls', the Biblical Books of Esther, Song of Songs, Ruth, Lamentations and Ecclesiastes

Chametz (*Cha'***metz**) Leaven, yeast

Chatan Bereshit (*Cha'***tan** *Be're'***shit**) The person called to the reading of the first Torah portion of the new cycle on Simchat Torah

Chatan Torah (*Cha'***tan** *To'***rah**) The person called to the reading of the last Torah portion of the old cycle on Simchat Torah

Chaver (*Cha'***ver**) A study companion

Chavruta (*Chav'roo'***ta**) A system of learning where two people study together

Chazan (*Cha'***zan**, pl. *Cha'zan'***im**) The person who leads prayers in the synagogue

Cheder (*Che'***der** or **Chay**'*der*) Religion classes for Jewish children

Chevra kaddisha (*Chev'***ra** *ka'dee'***sha**) Aramaic for sacred society, people who prepare a body for burial

Chevrat musar (*Chev'***rat** *mu'***sar**) Ethics group, people who meet to study Jewish ethical teachings

Chukim (*Choo'***kim**) Laws for which no reason is given; keeping these is seen as a test of faith

Chumash (*Chu'***mash**, pl. *Chu'mash'***im**) Short for 'chamishah chumshei Torah', a printed book of the Torah

Cohen (*Co'***hen**, pl. *Co'ha'***nim**) A priest

Dayanim (*Da'ya'***nim**, singular *Da'***yan**) Judges in a rabbinical court

Devarim (*De'var'***im**) Hebrew name for the Biblical Book of Deuteronomy

Diaspora 'Dispersion', the name given to Jews living outside Israel

Dreidle (*Drei'***dle**) (Yiddish) A spinning top with Hebrew letters used in a children's game during Hannukah

Druse Members of a political and religious sect of Muslims

Ellul (*El'***lul**) Sixth month of the Jewish year, in August/September

Etrog (*Et'***rog**) Citron, one of the four plant species used in the festival of Sukkot

Etz chaim (*Etz* **cha**'*yim*) 'Tree of life', the wooden rods to which the ends of the Torah scroll are stitched

Gabbai (*Ga'***bai**) Person responsible for organizing the synagogue service

Gaonim (*Ga'on'***im**, singular *Ga'***on**) 'Genius', Heads of the ancient academies

Gedaliah (*Ge'dal'***ya**) A day of fasting after Rosh Hashanah

Gemara (*Ge'ma'***ra**) Aramaic for 'learning', another name for the Talmud

Gemilut hassadim (*Ge'mil'***ut** *ha'sad'***im**) 'Acts of kindness' (see also tzedakah)

Get A document of divorce

Habad (*Ha'***bad**) Name of a group of Hasids, also called Lubevic

Hadassim (*Ha'da'***sim**) 'Branches of myrtle' one of the four plant species used in the festival of Sukkot

Haftarah (*Haf'ta'***rah**, pl. *Haf'ta'***rot**) A portion from the Books of the Prophets read on Sabbath morning after the sidra

Hagadah (*Ha'ga'***dah**, pl. *Ha'ga'***dot**) 'Telling', the book read during the seder meal on Passover

Hakotel Hamaaravi (*Ha'ko'***tel** *Ha'ma'ra'***vi**) The Western Wall of the Temple

Halakhah (*Ha'la'***khah**, pl. *Ha'la'***chot**) The name given to Jewish law

Hallel (*Ha'***lel**) 'Praise', Psalms 113 to 118

Hanukiah (*Cha'noo'***kee'***ah*) A nine-branched oil- or candle-holder lit during Hannukah

Hanukkah (*Cha'noo'***kah**) 'Dedication', an 8-day festival celebrating the rededication of the Temple in 165 BCE

Haroset (*Ha'***ro**'*set*) A mixture of apples, wine, nuts and spices eaten during the seder meal on Passover

Hasidic movement (*Ha'***sid**'*ic*) A Jewish revivalist movement that began during the seventeenth century

Hasidim (*Ha'sid'***im**, singular *Ha'***sid**) Members of the Hasidic movement

Haskalah (*Has'ka'***lah**) 'Enlightenment', a movement started by Jews who wanted to reduce the differences between Jews and non-Jews

Havdalah (*Hav'da'***lah**) 'Separation', a ceremony marking the end of Sabbath and festivals

Hechsher (*Hech'***sher**) A stamp or label certifying that a food product is kosher

Hibat Zion (*Hi'***bat** *Zi'***on**) 'Love of Zion', a political movement aiming to settle Jews in the Holy Land

Hillel (*Hi'***lel**) An important rabbi of the first century

Holocaust The murder of over 6 million Jews by Nazis in Europe 1933–1945

Hoshanah Rabbah (*Ho'sha'***nah** *Ra'***bah**) The seventh day of Sukkot

Hovovei Zion (*Ho'vo'***vei** *Zi'***on**) Members of Hibat Zion

Huppah (*Hoo'***pah**) 'Covering', the canopy under which a Jewish couple are married

Iyar (*I'***yar**) Second month of the Jewish year, in April/May

Kabbalah (*Ka'ba'***lah**) Jewish mysticism

Kaddish (*Ka'***dish**) Prayer or praise to God, said by a mourner

Kashrut (*Kash'***rut**) When food is kosher; study of laws relating to kosher food

Kedoshim (*Ke'dosh'***im**) 'Holy ones', Jewish martyrs

Ketubah (*Ke'too'***bah**) Marriage certificate or contract

Ketuvim (*Ke'too'***vim**) Hebrew name for the 'writings', the third section of the Hebrew Bible

Kibbutz (*Ki'***butz**, pl. *Ki'butz'***im**) A collective settlement where members share ownership

Kiddush (*Ki'***dush**) 'Sanctification', blessing recited over wine at the start of Sabbath and festival meals

Kiddush hashem (*Ki'***dush** *ha'***shem**) 'Sanctification of the name of God', sacrificing one's life for God

Kiddush Levanah (*Ki'***dush** *Le'va'***nah**) 'Sanctification of the moon', blessing recited during the first part of each Jewish month

Kiddushin (*Ki'dush'***in**) Marriage

Kinot (*Ki'***not**) 'Dirges', poems recited in the synagogue on Tisha b'Av

Kippah (*Ki'***pah**) Skull cap worn by Jewish males

Kittel (**Ki**'*tle*) White, smock-like garment worn by Jewish men on the Day of Atonement

Knesset (*K'***nes**'*et*) Israeli Parliament

Kol Nidrei (*Kol ni'***drey**) Annulment of vows made before the Day of Atonement service

Kollel (*Ko'***lel**) College of advanced rabbinical studies

Kosher (*Ko'***sher**) 'Fitting', food that a Jewish person is allowed to eat

Kupple (**Ku**'*ple*) Another name for kippah, skull cap worn by male Jews

Kvatter (**Kva**'*ter*) Yiddish word for 'bearer' – one of the people who carry a baby boy to and from his circumcision

Lag b'Omer (**Lag** *b'***O**'*mer*) 33rd day of the counting of the Omer (the time between Passover and Shavuot)

Lamdan (*Lam'***dan**) Torah scholar

Leshon hakodesh (*Les'***hon** *ha'***ko**'*desh*) Lit. 'the holy tongue'

Lulav (*Lu'***lav**) Palm branch, one of the four plant species used during Sukkot

Maarat Hamachpelah (*Ma'a'***rat** *Ha'mach'pe'***lah**) Cave where the Patriarchs and Matriarchs are buried

Machazit hashekel (*Ma'chaz'***it** *ha'***she**'*kel*) 'Half a shekel', name given to a donation towards the upkeep of the synagogue, made during the Fast of Esther

Magen David (*Ma'***gen** *Da'***vid**) Shield of David, a six-pointed star emblem

Mamzer (*Mam'***zer**, pl. *Mam'zer'***im**) A child born of an adulterous relationship

Mamzerut (*Mam'ze'***rut**) The condition of being a mamzer

Mashiach (*Ma'***shi**'*ach*) The Messiah

Maskilim (*Mas'kil'***im**) Followers of Haskalah

Matzah (*Mat'***zah** pl. *Mat'***zot**) Unleavened bread

Megillah (*Me'gil'***lah**) 'Scroll', name given to the Biblical Book of Esther

Melachot (*Me'lach'***ot**) The 39 types of work forbidden on the Sabbath

Menorah (*Me'no'***rah**) The seven-branched candle-holder used in the Temple

Mezuzah (*Me'zu'***zah**, pl. *Me'zu'***zot**) 'Doorpost', small parchment scroll fixed to the right-hand doorpost of rooms in a Jewish house (except bathroom and toilet)

Midrash (*Mid'***rash**, pl. *Mid'rash'***im**) Jewish writings that contain teachings illustrated with stories or parables

Migrash (*Mig'***rash**) Open land surrounding a town

Mikveh (*Mik'***veh**, pl. *Mik'va'***ot**) Immersion pool

Minchah (*Min'***chah**) The afternoon service

Minyan (*Min'***yan**) 'Required number', ten males over the age of 13 needed if certain prayers are to be said

Mishnah (*Mish'***nah**) 1. A work in 63 volumes compiled by Rabbi Judah the Prince (c. 200 CE) containing major rabbinical opinions. 2. Another name for the Biblical Book of Deuteronomy

Mishnah Torah (*Mish'***nah** *To'***rah**) A Jewish code of law written by Rabbi Moses Ben Maimon (Maimonides) in the thirteenth century

Mitzvah (*Mitz'***vah**, pl. *Mitz'***vot**) Commandment

Moed (*Mo'***ed**) 'Festival', the second division of the Mishnah

Mohel (*Mo'***hel**) A person who carries out circumcision

Moshav (*Mo'***shav**, pl. *Mo'shav'***im**) Settlement or village where people own their own property

Moshe Rabbenu (*Mo'***sheh** *Ra'***bey**'*noo*) Our teacher Moses

Musaf (*Mu'***saf**) The additional service

Musar movement (*Mu'***sar** or **Mu**'*sar*) A movement aimed to improve the character training of Jews

Nashim (*Na'***shim**) 'Women', the third section of the Mishnah

Neilah (*Ne'i'***lah**) 'Closing the gates', the closing service on the Day of Atonement

Ner tamid (*Ner ta'***mid**) 'Perpetual light', the light always kept burning in the synagogue

Nevi'im (*Ne'vi'***im**) 'Prophets', Hebrew name for the second section of the Hebrew Bible

Nezikin (*Ne'zi'***kin**) 'Damages', the fourth section of the Mishnah

Nidah (*Ni'***dah**) A woman who is menstruating

Nisan (*Ni'***san**) First month of the Jewish year, in March/April

Nisuin (*Ni'su'***in**) 'Elevation', marriage

Noachide Laws Code of law given to Noah in the Bible having seven principles that Jews regard as the basic rules of morality for all human beings

Omer (**O**'*mer*) A measure of barley; the name given to the period between Pesach and Shavuot

Onan (*O'***nan**) A mourner up until the time of the burial

Parev or **Parve** (*Par'ev, Par've*) 'Neutral', food that may be eaten either with meat or dairy foods

Pesach (**Pe**'*sach*) Passover

Pogroms Anti-Jewish riots

Purim (*Pur'***im**) Festival to remember the saving of the Jews from being killed in the time of Xerxes 1, King of Persia

Pushkes (**Push**'*kes*) (Yiddish) Collection boxes

Rabbi 'My master', the spiritual leader of a Jewish community

Rashi (**Ra**'*shi*) Rabbi Shlomoh Yitzchaki (1040–1105), important writer on Bible and Talmud

Rebbe (**Re**'*be*, pl. *Re*'**bei**'*im*) Leader of Hasidic group or movement

Rosh Chodesh (**Rosh Cho**'*desh*) 'Head of the month', the first day of a Jewish month

Rosh Hashanah (**Rosh** *Ha*'*sha*'**nah**) 'Head of the year', Jewish New Year

Sandek (*San'***dek**) The man who holds the baby boy during circumcision

Sanhedrin (*San'hed'***rin**) Supreme rabbinical court

Seder (**Se**'*der*, to rhyme with 'raider') 'Order', the Passover meal

Sefer Torah (*Se'***fer** *To'***rah**) 'Scroll of the Torah'

Selichot (*Se'lich'***ot**) 'Pardons', prayers for forgiveness

Sephardim (*Se'far'***dim**) Oriental Jews

Shabbat (*Sha'***bat**) Sabbath

Shabbat Mevarchim (*Sha'***bat** *Me'var'***chim**) 'Sabbath of blessing', the Sabbath preceding a new month

Shabbat Shalom (*Sha'***bat** *Sha'***lom**) 'Sabbath of Peace', a Hebrew greeting used on the Sabbath

Shabbos (**Sha**'*bos*) Western pronunciation of Shabbat

Shacharit (*Sha'char'***it**) The morning service

Shalom (*Sha'***lom**) Peace

Shamash (*Sha'***mash**) 'Servant'. 1. The person who sees that the synagogue is in order. 2. The candle used to light up the other candles or oil lamps of the hanukiah

Shatnez (*Shat'***nez**) 'Mixed stuff', mixture of linen and woollen fibres which may not be worn in the same garment

Shavuot (*Sha'vu'***ot**) 'Weeks', the festival of Pentecost

Shechitah (*She'chi'***tah**) Jewish method of animal slaughter

Shekel (**She**'*kel*) A Jewish coin

Sheloshim (*She'lo'***shim**) Lit. 'thirty', i.e. the month of mourning

Shema (*She'***mah**) 'Hear', Jewish prayer stating the oneness of God

Shemini Atzeret (*She'***mi**'**ni** *Atz'er'***et**) 'Assembly of the eighth day', a one-day festival at the end of Sukkot

Shemot (*She'***mot**) 'Names', the Hebrew name for the second Book of the Bible

Shevat (*She'***vat**) Eleventh month of the Jewish year, in January/February

Shiva (*Shi'***vah**) 'Seven', the first seven days after a funeral

Shiva b'rachot (*Shi'***va** *bra'***chot**) 'Seven blessings' recited at a Jewish wedding and after each feast during the first seven days after a marriage

Shoah (**Sho**'*ah*) 'Destruction', the Holocaust

Shochet (*Sho'***chet**) Slaughterer of animals

Shofar (*Sho'***far**) Hollowed-out ram's horn used to produce musical notes

Shul (rhymes with 'fool') Yiddish for synagogue

Shulchan Aruch (*Shul'***chan** *A'***ruch**) 'Table prepared', the code of Jewish law compiled by Rabbi Joseph Caro in the sixteenth century

Shushan Purim (*Shu'***shan** *Pu'***rim**) The day after Purim

Siddur (*Si'***dur** , pl. *Si'dur'***im**) Prayer book

Sidra (*Si'***drah**) A portion of the Torah read in the synagogue on Sabbath mornings

Simchat Torah (*Sim'***chat** *To'***rah**) Rejoicing of the Law

Sivan (*Si'van*) The third month of the Jewish year

Sofer (*So'fer*, pl. *So'fer'im*) A scribe

Sukkah (*Su'kah*) 'Covering', the temporary shelter covered with leaves that Jewish people live in during the festival of Sukkot

Sukkot (*Su'kot*) 1. The festival that remembers the trek of the ancient Israelites through the desert. 2. Plural of sukkah

Taharah (*Ta'ha'rah*) Purity

Taharat hamishpacha (*Ta'ha'rat ha'mish'pa'chah*) 'Family purity', Jewish laws regulating sexual relations

Taharot (*Ta'ha'rot*) Fifth section of the Mishnah

Tallit (*Ta'lit*, pl. *ta'li'tot*) 'Robe', woollen or silk robe worn by Jewish males during morning prayers.

Tallit gadol (*Ta'lit ga'dol*) 'Large robe', full name for tallit

Tallit katan (*Ta'lit ka'tan*) 'Small robe', worn by Jewish males during daytime

Talmud (*Tal'mud*) Collection of writings of Jewish law and ethical teachings compiled about 500 CE

Talmud Torah (*Tal'mud To'rah*, Western pronunciation) Jewish religion classes

Tammuz (*Ta'muz*) Fourth month of the Jewish year, in June/July

Tashlich (*Tash'lich*) 'Casting away', a service recited near a river at the Jewish New Year

Tefillin (*Te'fi'lin*, singular *Te'fi'lah*) The two leather boxes containing Biblical verses written on parchment scrolls. Jewish males wear them at morning prayers on week days

Tenakh (*Te'nakh*) Hebrew name for the Bible

Tevet (*Te'vet*) Tenth month of the Jewish year, in December/January

Tikkun olam (*Ti'kun o'lam*) Correcting the world, i.e. improving society

Tisha b'Av (*Ti'sha be'Av*) Ninth of Av, a fast day to remember the destruction of the Temple and other tragedies

Tishrei (*Tish'rey*) Seventh month of the Jewish year, in September/October

Torah (*To'rah*) 'Instruction', name given by Jews to the first five Books of the Bible, sometimes to the whole of the Bible, and sometimes to all rabbinic literature

Tosafot (*To'sa'fot*) Additions; commentaries on the Talmud

Tosefta (*To'sef'ta*) 'Addition', a collection of rabbinic opinions omitted from the Mishnah

Treifah (*Trey'fah*) 'Torn', the opposite of kosher, i.e. not permitted

Tumah (*Tu'mah*) 'Impurity'

Tzedakah (*Tze'dah'kah*) 'Righteousness', act of giving money to a worthy cause (see also gemilut hassadim)

Tzizit (*Tzi'zit*) 'Fringes', the tassels on each corner of the tallit gadol and tallit katan

Vayikra (*Va'yik'rah*) 'And he called', Hebrew name for the third Book of the Bible

Yad Vashem (**Yad Va***'shem*) The Holocaust Memorial Centre in Jerusalem

Yarmulke (**Yar***'mul'ke*) (Yiddish) A skull cap worn by religious males; also called a kippah

Yarzheit (**Yar***'tzite*) Yiddish term for the anniversary of a death

Yeshivot (*Ye'shi'vot*, singular *Ye'shi'va*) 'Place of sitting', Talmudic academies

Yichud (*Yi'chud*) 'Togetherness', the moments following a wedding when bride and groom are together in private

Yiddish (**Yid***'dish*) Language spoken by some western Jews, similar to German

Yom Ha'atzmaut (**Yom** *Ha'atz'ma'ut*) Israel Independence Day

Yom Hashoah (**Yom** *Ha'sho'ah*) Holocaust Remembrance Day

Yom Kippur (**Yom** *Ki'pur*) Day of Atonement

Yom Yerushalayim (**Yom** *Ye'ru'sh'lai'im*) Jerusalem Day

Zeraim (*Ze'ra'im*) The first section of the Mishnah

Zeved habat (*Ze'***ved** *ha'***bat**) 'The gift of a daughter', a naming ceremony for girls in Sephardi communities

Zion (*Tzi'***on**) Originally one of the names of Jerusalem, also used as a name for the Holy Land

Zohar (*Zo'***har**) The most important writings of Jewish mystics

INDEX